# Challenged

from here
to eternity

# Challenged
## from here to eternity

*Recognizing and defeating threats
to a strong faith*

# SHERI WALKER

Walking Turtle Press

To Mike, through all the ups and
downs of life, you've been my
relief, my support, and the love
and kindness I've relied on for
over 40 years.

# Contents


Introduction .......................................................................... 9

**SECTION 1: A NEW CHALLENGE** ....................................... 13
  1 - The Spotted Lanternfly's Deception ............................. 15
  2 - The Great Mediator ................................................... 25

**SECTION 2: THE CHALLENGE OF EMOTIONS** ................. 33
  3 - Feelings: A Worthy Demotion ..................................... 35
  4 - Fear: The Dreaded Awful ............................................ 45
  5 - Control: By God's Design ............................................ 54
  6 - Shame: A Call Unanswered ......................................... 62
  7 - Anger: The Bitter End ................................................ 72
  8 - Comfort: An Addiction to Avoid ................................. 82
  9 - Perfectionism: A New 80/20 Rule ............................... 92

**SECTION 3: THE CHALLENGE OF CIRCUMSTANCE** ........ 101
  10 - Under His Care ....................................................... 103
  11 - How to Survive the Sifting ...................................... 113
  12 - No Tidy Endings ..................................................... 126

**SECTION 4: THE CHALLENGE OF CULTURE** ................. 135
  13 - Flee For Your Life ................................................... 137
  14 - An Un-Moderate Life .............................................. 147

**SECTION 5: FINAL CHALLENGES** ................................... 159
  15 - Put On the Cape ..................................................... 161
  16 - Hope Deferred ....................................................... 170
  17 - A Worthy Promotion ............................................... 180

Epilogue: The Frailty of a Foreigner ................................... 189
Acknowledgements ............................................................. 193
About Sheri Walker .............................................................. 194
About From Here to Eternity Series ..................................... 196

# Introduction

Dear Friend,

I'm rarely inclined to read introductions. Nonetheless, I have one for you. It's a letter to you, new and old friends, because that's how I see us; friends who I know personally, or know me through my first book, and new friends who are joining me on this journey.

The content of this book, *Challenged*, was originally placed in my first book, *Strong, From Here to Eternity*. I soon realized the challenges (or threats) to a strong faith are many, and I wanted to give them the time and depth they deserved. I trust you'll see yourself in the ones I've tackled, or like me, you'll have experienced all of them to some degree. I hope you'll ponder them, gain new perspective, and grow a desire to consider the threats (or strongholds) in your own faith walk, as I have.

A friendly warning that this book is for you, and not for anyone else in your life. It's not about seeing weaknesses or strongholds in others. We don't want to be rebuked by God for "looking for the speck of sawdust in your brother's eye, while paying no attention to the plank in your own eye" (Matt. 7:3–5, emphasis added). We all have enough "planks" to go around and it's best we focus on ourselves. There was a time almost twenty years ago when I confessed to a friend the problems my husband, Mike, and I were having with our adopted daughters' behaviors. My friend failed to listen with *plankless* ears, as she told me, "Give them to me for a couple of weeks. I'll turn them around and fix them for you." Boy, did I want to take her up on her offer. Her harsh words, meant to elevate herself, gave me shame and put me on the defensive. With a forced smile, I ended our conversation quickly, telling myself she had no idea how hurtful her words were. I didn't need anyone treating me as if I wasn't a good enough parent. I felt like one all on my own. No one needs you to criticize or fix them. We have enough trouble fixing ourselves.

As in my first book, I'm intent on having us train for godliness. Paul talks about this often in the many epistles (or letters) he wrote in the New Testament. Life is a daily battle to fight well, and I want to help you in the fight.

All this talk about fighting and strongholds can be exhausting, and at times, I've relieved some of the pressure with a little self-deprecating humor. I occasionally take jabs at myself, especially in the chapters on fear, comfort, moderation, control, and well, you get the picture. It's not difficult to find a bit of humor in the depths of our strongholds. This doesn't mean they aren't topics to be taken seriously. Honestly, I find most everything serious or I wouldn't write about them. My family will tell you firsthand I'm no comedian (I don't understand most jokes), but there's a place for recognizing our ineptitudes with some humor. A little humor goes further than a hammer, although I can be good with a hammer, if given the opportunity. I've found a hammer, however, rarely does the trick. I hope you'll see my stories as relatable, and not walk in shame.

Lastly, a warning about death. It's a common theme for me. Eternity is my destiny and has become more profound because I have faced death, and addressing it is normal. I don't think the topic of death should be swept under the rug. I find it natural to talk about, and I hope you will find it to be a natural upbeat theme in my writings. I want to inspire as we seek to live *and* die well. This is not for an aging crowd only. This is for us all to recognize, because the earlier we view our lives through an eternal lens, the better off we'll be. And, as I've experienced, life passes by so very quickly.

The teacher is the best learner. One of my favorite things about writing every day is that it forces me to be a better steward of the Word. You can't deep dive into a subject, see what God says about it, think on it, write about it, and not do the necessary work. I'm finding my heart leans more and more to wanting others to seek God's Word for themselves. There's such beauty, surprise, redemption, truth, and power in it.

If you've made it this far in the often-unread introduction, I want to tell you I've prayed for you. I write with you in mind. I consider the young, the married, the un-married, the moms, the not-yet-or-never-will-be moms, the careered, the middle-aged, and the elderly. That's a large demographic, but as a woman in her sixties, I've been in all those shoes at one time or another (I'm not yet elderly). Mostly, I consider that you, my new and old friends, will be searching and will have a desire to discover new truths in your walk with God.

"Teach the Believers Darling, Teach the Believers."[1]

I love this saying from Jim Elliot to his wife, Elisabeth, when she asked what she would do if he didn't return from his mission. Jim, along with four other men, went to bring the good news of the gospel to the Aucas, a tribe in Ecuador known for their brutal killings. Despite the Aucas' brutal history, the five missionary men were eager to convert them. They left on January 3rd, 1956. They never returned. They were speared to death by the Aucas early in their mission.

Jim Elliot's last words to Elisabeth have been words I've clung to as I've considered my own mission of discipleship. I've suffered and survived many things. Trauma. Illness. Debilitation. Loss. I believe it's because of my suffering (and of course, a growing faith) that I'm on the path I'm now on, and it's the words of Jim Elliot which so often ring in my head. *Teach the Believers Darling, Teach the Believers.*

I hope you can relate to my stories, and I hope you run to God's Word as the anchor for it all. I hope you take the time to dive into the *Study and Reflection* section after each chapter. I don't want to spoon feed ideas without you testing to see if

---

[1] https://www.reviveourhearts.com/podcast/revive-our-hearts/motivated-his-glory/

they're God's ideas. I want to inspire an interest and love in Jesus and his Word. That's the moment I'll succeed in my writing.

I'm here being challenged right beside you, running and striving towards God who, as Elisabeth Elliot said all the time, "loves you with an everlasting love." Let's lead with this in mind as we explore the depths of the threats which challenge to steal our bodies, hearts, minds, and the strong faith we seek.

Your friend in Christ,
Sheri

# Section 1

# A NEW CHALLENGE

*"He gives strength to the weary and increases the power of the weak. Even youths grow tired and weary, and young men stumble and fall; but those who hope in the LORD will renew their strength. They will soar on wings like eagles; they will run and not grow weary, they will walk and not be faint."*
Isaiah 40:29–31

# 1

# The Spotted Lanternfly's Deception

*I started to hate them, because once you know,
it's impossible to love them.*

The Spotted Lanternfly is an insect of great beauty. Its blood red, beige, and black spotted wingspan looks more like a tribal headdress than something you'd find on an insect in your backyard. Despite their beauty, however, they are an invasive and dreaded insect, and one day they showed up unexpected and uninvited.

In the spring of 2022, Mike and I discovered a handful of cute, small, white-spotted black bugs we'd never seen before. In a couple of weeks, a few more of them appeared, and we learned they were the infamous Spotted Lanternfly, in their immature nymph stage. We'd never seen one but read about them coming to Central Pennsylvania. Their infestation and reputation for destroying crops and trees is so devastating, local officials encourage ridding as many as you can. At the nymph stage, they don't yet have wings, are slow moving, and easy to kill. I could squash dozens at a time, and quickly became a crazy nymph-squashing machine. Eventually, as the days turned to weeks, it felt like a futile task as their numbers and size grew larger than my capacity to keep up.

It became apparent that my efforts were only scratching the surface as I watched neighbors catch (literally) tens of thousands on three-foot-wide sticky tape placed on their larger trees. The nymphs, now full-flight insects, stuck to the tape in such thick clusters you couldn't see the yellow tape behind them. The Spotted Lanternfly had become my nemesis, and I started to hate them, because once you *know*, it's impossible to love them.

This invasive insect is the perfect analogy for our Christian lives, and it's the heart of the messages in this book. There are things which look attractive but threaten our strong faith walk with God. We aren't always aware of the devastating effects because of the attractive lure they present and the slow creeping pace at which they enter our lives and grow out of control.

## EMOTIONS, CIRCUMSTANCES, AND CULTURE

What are these lures (or strongholds) which threaten us? I've placed them in three categories: emotions, circumstances, and culture. Some of them happen to us and we have little control over them, but I contend that all of them come with a choice in how we respond. Some may be controversial, and although I don't like controversy or conflict, I've tried not to shy away from at least the start of a discussion. Discussion is good and worthy if it leads us to the right source.

If I had to pick one of the three categories I'm most passionate about, it would be dealing scripturally with *EMOTIONS* (no pun intended). I consider it among our greatest and most worthy challenges to honor our emotions (or feelings) as the gift they are, while keeping them in check within the boundaries of scriptural truths. It's a tricky balance, but it's in the daily dying to oneself, and following Jesus where you will find strength and a growing heart of joy. We are accustomed to thinking of joy as an emotion, but it is much deeper than that. Joy is a fruit of the Spirit, a characteristic of God, a state of being in our Christian life, *and* an emotion all wrapped into one. For the mature believer, lasting joy is undeterred by difficult circumstances and is a worthy calling to be embraced and nurtured.

The next category of strongholds to explore is *CIRCUMSTANCES*. Circumstances can be within our control or outside of our control. I focus mainly on circumstances we would consider unfavorable and difficult, regardless of whether we could have prevented, changed, or guided them differently. Because I have experienced many hardships, I explore how we view our circumstances, what they mean in the life of a believer, and how to overcome what we think we can't overcome.

And finally, while a large part of me would like to steer clear of social commentary, I think it's relevant for every believer to address the strongholds of *CULTURE* as they pertain to biblical truth. In fact, I think it's negligent not to. If we don't head off the threat of cultural deceptions, we'll be forever caught in the traps of sin and evil.

All three categories; emotions, circumstances, and culture overlap. They don't neatly reside within their own parameters, even as I have attempted to place them there. Circumstances incite emotions. Emotions dictate circumstances. Our lives happen within our culture, culture being both *micro*-culture (our own small environments like family, neighborhood, or church), or *macro*-culture (our society and the world at large). We are a subset of our cultures, and hold certain beliefs within them, and make decisions accordingly. As we explore these categories, my hope is that God's Word will shine through as our final authority and reduce the gray matter in our lives. What is gray matter you ask? Good question.

## GRAY MATTER

The decisions we make are not always black and white. They may not be clearly addressed in the Bible, may not have a clear path, or are not the same from person to person. Many of our decisions are gray, and because they are, we are to continually search God's Word, pray for guidance, and press our lives into righteous living. I'm not here to provide a checklist of the good and the bad, as if they could be placed into two columns. It is for you to walk through the gray areas of life and make decisions that are in your best interests to walk in holiness and righteousness.

As an example, one of our gray matters showed up throughout our family life when Mike and I determined where to send our four daughters to school each year. During their schooling years, they went to public school, Christian school, charter school, Co-op (or Cooperative Education), Montessori, therapeutic schools, and/or were homeschooled. There were no checklists to tell Mike and I where to send them each year, nor would I tell anyone else what they should do about their schooling choices. Some probably thought us a little crazy (and more than a little wrong) for the constant changes we made, but Mike and I prayed yearly, and left each year's leading for each daughter open to change if necessary. We did our best to stay in God's will, not our own. Whether we made all the right decisions is not something we look back on. We did our best, we had a desire to do God's will, and we felt called for each year's decisions. His grace was, and still is, sufficient for those particular choices or *gray matters*.

The grays of life's daily decisions will become easier to navigate once you're in the Word and practice continual discernment. It doesn't mean your decisions will be easy, but they will become less ambivalent and clearer. Whether to place a parent in a nursing home, homeschool your children, go vegan, hire someone to cut your grass, vacation at the beach every year, watch a police drama, or retire at sixty-five, and so forth. All these gray decisions vie for our attention but may not have clear-cut answers. Some of them are obviously not as impactful as others, but they all require some level of decision-making.

If you've read my first book, *Strong*, you know that no decision is benign to me. I challenge you to think intentionally that everything we do is important and has value one way or another. Proverbs 5:21 says, "Your ways are in full view of the LORD, and he examines all your paths." God examines *all* our paths. Shouldn't we as well?

Of course, there is black and white. You shouldn't steal. You should pay your bills. You should stop at a red light. You shouldn't hit anybody. They are clear in the Bible and clear in our laws. Black and white, however, is becoming more and more muddied into gray, and our discernment more confusing. I'm not making a political commentary. You'd not find many people less political than me. This isn't about politics or culture, per se. It's about being and staying in the Word so our knowing is clearer, our decisions stronger, and our closeness to God ever increasing. That's it. That's what life (and this book) is all about. All I'm asking you to do is read and consider, and then, ask the questions and seek the answers for yourself.

## BENEFICIAL TO WHO?

God's Word says, "while some things are permissible, not everything is beneficial" (1 Cor. 10:23). We want everything in our lives to be beneficial. Beneficial to who or what? Ourselves? No, beneficial to God's glory and his kingdom here on earth. Whatever decisions we make, we want to land on whatever opens us and others up to a relationship with Jesus and follow God in all things. We want our heart's desires to flow always in his direction. We want to be open and led by the Spirit in *all* things. Training is ongoing when it comes to how we conduct our lives.

The point of this book is to challenge us (you and me) to see, know, filter, discern, and steward our lives within the confines of a strong biblical foundation. And, most of all, trust and obey the one who seeks our trust and obedience. If you have accepted and know Jesus as your Savior, you were bought with a price. You are not your own. You are considerably less independent than our society would have you think. As a Christ follower, we are free to choose, but if we are obedient to God and his Word, we can't do what we want. Well… we *can*, but there will be consequences.

## THE THING WHICH DIRECTS THE HAND

As we delve into discovering the threats to our faith, we need to be careful how we determine what is and what isn't a challenge. We often see the circumstances in our lives as the threats themselves. Circumstances are often the things we can't change. We aren't necessarily looking to (nor can we) rid ourselves of most of our difficult circumstances. If circumstances could prevent strongholds, we could cut down our trees thereby ridding us forever of Spotted Lanternflies. That would be ridiculous. It's not the trees that need to be eliminated. They are only the circumstances drawing the Spotted Lanternflies to them, and not themselves inherently bad.

An aging parent is a circumstance, as is an illness. Having children who don't fit into a normal school environment, or a boss who gaslights you at every turn are circumstances. Granted, they are difficult circumstances, but how you respond within those circumstances either builds up or tears down the fortitude of your faith and the faith of others around you. The gaslighting boss isn't well-liked, and you and your co-workers bash her at every turn. Therein enters the slippery slope threatening to bring *you* down, not because of your boss's gaslighting, but because of your sinful response to it. There are many circumstances in life which threaten a strong faith, and we can recognize and deal with them *before* they capture our hearts.

In Matthew 5:30, Jesus said, "If your right hand causes you to stumble, cut it off and throw it away. It is better for you to lose one part of your body than for your whole body to go into hell." This strong language from Jesus is called hyperbole or an exaggerated statement for emphasis. He's not encouraging you to cut off your hand. He's not telling you to remove that which gives you the challenge, because it's not the hand God wants to deal with. It's the thing directing the hand and making decisions for it, the heart. It's the heart, along with the mind, which lacks trust and obedience, sometimes not even knowing who God is and what he says. Ignorance is not an excuse, even while we'd like to linger in it.

What presents itself as a devastating circumstance is often the very thing God uses to refine, change, mold, and grow our faith. The circumstances aren't the culprits or our downfall, it's how we interpret those circumstances, our responses to them, and our success (and failure) in filtering them through God's Word.

## A NEW CHALLENGE

Threats, like those tiny nymphs, come to infect, take over, confuse, and destroy. This is Satan's plan. There is an evil in this world waiting to bring us down, one little nymph at a time, which is why they are worthy to be considered, studied, combatted, and dealt with. We need to get rid of and ward off as many threats as we can before their devastation causes us harm, before they turn into full-fledged lanternflies, and become difficult, if not impossible, to eliminate.

In this book, I have taken on some of life's challenges, the ones I have experienced and/or continue to experience, and the ones I consider common to most of us. I pray you will see hope and not condemnation working through these challenges with me. I hold no condemnation, even for myself in my own challenges, only a deep desire to seek God's face, know his heart as he reveals it, and change my behaviors and desires accordingly.

These aren't the only challenges, but hopefully, they will start you thinking about specific challenges within your own life. I promise we all have them. If you are a Christ follower living in this world, you will have to wade through many challenges and gray areas.

I previously wrote *Strong, From Here to Eternity*, a partner to this book. The first chapter in the book gives a charge to journey together to be a stronger, unexpected, redefined, godly version of ourselves. A charge to stand firm and be *righteous and as bold as a lion* (Proverbs 28:1). It is a proactive challenge to seek God and steward your life for him.

This book is also a proactive charge, but in reverse. Instead of being on the attack, it is a challenge to move away from the threats (and sins) that leave us weak in our faith. In 1ˢᵗ Timothy 6:20, Paul says to Timothy, "Guard what has been entrusted to your care." If we consider this verse, we ask ourselves, "what is it that's been entrusted to our care?" Everything the Lord has given us. Our bodies. Our minds. Our families. Our faith. Our work. Our days. Everything. There's nothing outside his care. So, we ask ourselves, "how do we guard what has been entrusted to our care?" It's a two-fold approach.

Job 28:28 says, "The fear of the Lord is true wisdom; to forsake evil is real understanding." Turn away from evil and bad. Turn toward God and good. Fear (or respect and honor) of God works in tandem with forsaking evil. Both bring a growing wisdom, a gained strength, and a true joy in the Lord.

## IT WILL TAKE COURAGE

As in my first book, I encourage you to be "bold as a lion," because it will take boldness and courage, perhaps more courage to cut off threats than to seek strength. I can't keep my body healthy and fit without rejecting the things which make it weak, such as laziness, over-indulgence, and unhealthy food choices. I can't encourage patience and kindness within me if I care more about fairness and being right. I can't experience peace and trust if I grasp for control and let worry and anxiety threaten to overcome my thoughts. I can't obtain goodness while saturating myself in sin. I can't, and neither can you.

This is our new challenge. Run, don't walk, as we seek God's Word as the last word, certainly not mine or anyone else's. Be proactive in knowing what specific things threaten your faith so you can start rejecting them. Eventually, like those cute little nymphs, once you *know* what's not good for you, it will be impossible to love them. My hope is that we will recognize and hate the threats for what they are.

This new challenge won't be an easy one, but I promise it will be worth it. Ask Jesus, who is right now interceding for you and me, that "His grace be poured out abundantly on you, along with the faith and love that are in Him" (1 Tim. 1:14). Let the squashing begin.

# CHAPTER 1

## Study and Reflection

Bible verse: *Colossians 3:17* – Read.
Write out in the space below:

___________________________________________

___________________________________________

___________________________________________

___________________________________________

There are times I feel like an overzealous Jesus freak. I keep those overzealous feelings to myself (mostly). I don't let on to just anyone how I think because I don't want to scare people off with my intensity, and the older I get, the more intense I am becoming. This verse in Colossians is overzealous, and if we truly ponder it and take it to heart, it's not easy to digest.

So, let's analyze this overzealous directive from Paul in his letter to the Christians of Colossae.

Firstly, know that Paul's letters are addressed to other believers. It's mostly recognized that Paul wrote thirteen letters (not every biblical scholar agrees on this), and he wrote them to believers. One of his main missions was to build up the church: "And everything we do dear friends is for your strengthening" (2nd Cor. 12:19).

Why do you think it's important we know that Paul wrote Colossians 3:17 to believers?

What are the things in your own life that Paul wants you to "do in the name of the Lord Jesus." (You may answer directly from the text, "whatever you do," but consider a typical day and write out some of the things you do in that *typical* day.)

What would it look like for you to eat, drink, sleep, watch TV, discipline your kids, talk with your husband, clean the house, get the mail, take a walk, chat with a friend (are you getting the picture?) if you did it "in the name of Jesus?"

Whose name do we mostly run our day through? If you answered *you*, you'd be right. I struggle not putting me in the middle of my day, every day, all day.

Is the thought of doing everything in the name of Jesus a little overwhelming?

Can you take at least one thing in your day (perhaps brushing your teeth or having your first cup of coffee) and start to do it in the name of Jesus? It's going to feel odd, but like anything in life, practice is valuable. Practice seeing Jesus in your day and he'll honor that seeing. The point of this book is to challenge us (you and me) to see, know, filter, discern, and steward our lives within the confines of a strong faith in Jesus, as we turn towards him and away from sin.

> *Lord, we thank you for your Word which directs us to see you in all aspects of our daily lives. We dedicate this chapter, this book, and our day-to-day lives in your name. We search for truth as we seek your face, a worthy journey, and a defeat of anything that takes us away from you. Yet your will be done. Amen.*

2

# The Great Mediator

*I couldn't do it on my own. God got my attention.*

I know a thing or two about needing a mediator. It's called therapy, and Mike and I have done about 500 hours of it.  I figured out the approximate hours per week and weeks per years we invested in the outside therapeutic assistance of others. It's mind-boggling how many counselors, psychologists, psychiatrists, residential care providers, school counselors, and social services we saw in and out of our home. How many would it take to overcome the anger, rage, deceit, and aggression and heal our daughters' trauma? The aggression was ongoing and daily in some form or another. How often was I scared? How long would I live behind a locked bedroom door at night? The stress of it eventually became too much for me to handle. I needed relief.

When you have nowhere to turn, when you can't do it on your own, you turn to others for help. We needed others more than they knew. Some mediators were amazing. Some were good. Some were less than helpful. All were appreciated because they showed up. Mike and I were desperate for anyone who would help our pain and keep the girls and us safe.

I grew up thinking I was a strong person. There was nothing I couldn't do. My family's background was in construction, and they were hard working "can do" people. They taught me how to be a "can do" person. But the hardships and losses stacking up in adulthood showed me I wasn't strong enough on my own. I wasn't tough enough to fix everything the way my dad used to fix a broken toilet or replace the water heater. My own strength was not enough to prevent loss, trauma, and fear in my life.

Over the years, trauma and suffering seemed to have my name written all over it. Four miscarriages in my thirties. Losing my mother to breast cancer when I was thirty-nine. Our younger daughters' adoptive attachment and trauma struggles. A debilitating brain tumor when I was fifty-five. I'll admit it took a lot to get my attention and finally give in to God. I mean really give in, confess, and lay it all down and admit I couldn't do it on my own anymore. I needed a Savior to carry me through the rest of my days.

## I DON'T WANT TO BE GOD

At the end of myself, in the midst of great struggle, I found myself at a crossroad. I felt like Bruce (i.e. Jim Carrey) in *Bruce Almighty*, when God finally captures his attention. There's the climactic scene when Bruce is out in the pouring rain, and we see him falling on his knees in complete despair. In his sorrow and suffering, he comes to the end of himself, and he cries out to God, "You win. I'm done. Please. I don't want to do this anymore. I don't want to be God. I want you to decide what's right for me. I surrender to your will." Cue the uplifting music and the bright white light shining on Bruce's face which turns out to be an eighteen-wheeler truck. Bruce gets run over, dies, and finds himself in heaven with Morgan Freeman who is God. Well…I guess a Jim Carrey movie can't be too serious, but you get the picture. Bruce is undone and surrenders himself. It's a beautiful scene and one I relate to.

I couldn't do it on my own. God got my attention. I knew I needed to turn my heart completely over to God's will, no matter where it led. I needed Christ to save me from myself and be the loving and mediating Savior of my life. We recognize our need for a Savior when we recognize our need to be saved.

In Job 9:33–35 (NLT), Job says, "If only there were a mediator between us [Job and God], someone who could bring us together. The mediator could make God stop beating me, and I would no longer live in terror of his punishment. Then I could speak to him without fear, but I cannot do that in my own strength."

Job, a "blameless man," was struck hard with the loss of his children, his animals, his possessions, his respectful position in society, and finally, his health. He is completely beaten down. His wife is bitter. His friends are critical. They repeatedly tell Job he brought his horrible circumstances on himself by his unrecognized and unrepentant sin. The book of Job is a strange anomaly for me, and I fail to understand all of it, but oh what treasures it has, and "if only there were a mediator" is one of them. Job didn't know there would indeed be that person one day.

## A MEDIATOR AND GREAT INTERCESSOR

In *Strong, From Here to Eternity*, I ended the book exploring Jesus as our Master Shepherd and we as the defenseless sheep who follow him. In this book, I'm switching gears to see another side of Jesus, our Mediator, an intercessory who acts and prays on behalf of his followers. It's unfathomable that Jesus does this for us. He's working right alongside the Holy Spirit to reform our hearts, transform our lives, and intercede to the Father on our behalf. He loved us enough to die on the cross for me and for you, and he's still at work in our lives.

1st Timothy 2:5 says, "For there is one God and one mediator between God and mankind, the man Christ Jesus, who gave himself as a ransom for all people."

In this book, I explore many threats we need to be aware of, but we can't beware on our own. We need an intercessor, a mediator to help us. Jesus *and* the Holy Spirit convict, save, guide, and advocate for us. "And I will ask the Father, and he will give you another Advocate [Holy Spirit] to help you and be with you forever" (John 14:16). And John 14:26 says, "But the Advocate, the Holy Spirit, whom the

Father will send in my name, will teach you all things and will remind you of everything I have said to you."

## WE CAN'T MANIPULATE GOD

What does this all mean? It means we are to become holy, set apart, and devoted to God and the truths of the Word, but we can't do it on our own. We can't contrive a plan to beware of threats on our own, nor can we have a safety net of good works to save us from our problems. This kind of thinking defines the prosperity gospel, and it is a false gospel. It says God is good to the good and bad to the bad. No. No. No. That is not a biblical solution to how life is going to turn out for those who are in Jesus Christ.

The idea that we can manipulate our own destiny takes Jesus out of the equation. Isn't that the problem Jesus had with the pharisees? *Their* knowledge and *their* wisdom took God out of the equation of *their* holiness. They were not humble enough to see God as the one who not only understands life's math but is in control of it. They didn't see their need of God. They didn't call it the prosperity gospel, but it seems to me this was the inception of it. It's just been repackaged over the years.

Job is a clear example of why the prosperity gospel (good health and wealth procreated by one's good faith) should be thrown out. He was a good man who had horrible things happen to him. Job's friends criticize him, believing it was Job's sin which caused his tragedies and suffering. They urge him to repent of his sin. It was Job's failing, they argue, that brought his demise. However, it was God himself who called Job faithful and blameless. The biblical story proves we can't manipulate God for health and wealth by what we do, nor can we be good enough to avoid problems.

## THE SUFFERING GOSPEL

No one was more faithful than Job and yet God allowed Satan's attacks on him. God is God. He has a plan, and his plan is carried out in Job's suffering, even if I can't understand all its complexities. Let us swallow that hard pill.

It's through Job (and others) we see tangibly that God allows, ordains, and predestines us for suffering. While not something we want to hear, Scripture is clear that once we enter our position of saved by the blood of Jesus and accept his gift of grace, we enter a kind of suffering gospel.

Paul tells us in Philippians 1:29, "For it has been granted to you on behalf of Christ not only to believe in him, but also to suffer for him," or in the KJV, "to suffer for his sake." It says we have been granted this right to suffer. I think of being granted something as a positive thing, but I don't see suffering as a positive thing. I don't know about you, but I didn't get into Christianity to be granted suffering. That's not what I signed up for. I wanted bells and whistles, and some grandeur in my life. Yes, I wanted Jesus, but I wanted protection and goodness and splendor and everything that comes with Jesus. The good news is we have that too.

Yet we suffer. We hurt. And more of the same over and over. It's our destiny. And hopefully, we turn to God and ask for relief. We give our will over to him. That's our ultimate call and like Bruce, with our suffering, we may find we are at the end of ourselves, as we plead with God, "You win. I'm done. Please. I don't want to do this anymore. I don't want to be God. I want you to decide what's right for me. I surrender to your will."

I hope you'll start here, with Jesus. He is there to save us and along with the Holy Spirit, carry the yoke when we suffer and "intercede to the Father on our behalf in accordance with the will of God" (Rom. 8:27, emphasis added).

God *can* strengthen us. We *can* grow in the Word. We *can* recognize sin for what it is, and we *can* run away from it as we run toward a God who enables us. It's *our* work to do, but nothing, if not done to God's glory, and under the authority of his will is worthwhile. In the end, if we abide in Jesus and seek the will of God, we will prosper. So, I suppose there *is* a prosperity gospel of sorts, and it's found in the person of Jesus Christ. He is our destiny, the grandeur we seek, and our final perfect ending, here and forevermore.

# CHAPTER 2

## Study and Reflection

Bible verse: *1 Timothy 2:5* – Read.
Write out in the space below:

_______________________________________________

_______________________________________________

_______________________________________________

_______________________________________________

Define mediator (google the Hebrew definition):

_______________________________________________

_______________________________________________

You might have found the words, *Reconciler* and/or *Intercessor*. Look them up and define what they mean and also, how they differ?

There are many words in the New Testament (especially) which define who Jesus is and what he does on our behalf: Saves. Reckons. Intercedes. Mediates. Advocates.

What do they all mean? Are they the same? How do they differ?

The truth is, we could spend a long time studying and deconstructing the differences and nuances of each of them, but John 14:6 says it best, "Jesus answered. I am the way and the truth and the life. No one comes to the Father except through me."

Jesus saves, prays, petitions, reckons, intercedes, mediates, advocates, and draws us to the Father. Jesus is persistent in his love and his efforts wanting all to come to know him. Wanting all to come to God, the Father. Wanting all to be saved.

That's the kind of mediator I want on my side. One that seeks me out because he loves me that much.

What about you? Can you see your need for a mediator who loves you this much? What kind of things do you want Jesus to go to the Father for on your behalf? (HINT: It must align with biblical truths)

Have you considered these aspects of Jesus' character before? (And isn't it all so amazing?)

> *Dear Jesus, thank you for loving us so much that you seek us out. Thank you for reconciling us on the cross so that we too can be with God; so that he is made approachable to us. Help us to understand what we can sometimes make so complicated. Thank you for your patience to wait for all to come to a saving knowledge of you. This alone is worth every hard thing we must go through. Yet your will be done. Amen.*

# THE CHALLENGE OF EMOTIONS

*"For the Word of God is alive and active. Sharper than any double-edged sword, it penetrates even to dividing soul and spirit, joints, and marrow; it judges the thoughts and attitudes of the heart."*
Hebrews 4:12

# 3

## Feelings: A Worthy Demotion

*It took him three days to get over my indulgent wrongdoing.*

I met Mike's family on the heels of impulse. Impulse is a strong urge to do something, and I was well-accustomed to following them, especially in my younger years. We were in college, were newly in love, and Mike had gone home for a long weekend. I missed him and wanted to be with him. I was supposed to be running in a track meet, but I made up an excuse about not feeling well, and for the first time ever, I skipped a meet. I somehow hitched a ride with the men's baseball team, who happened to be playing close to Mike's hometown. When the team arrived at the field, I found a payphone (in the days of no cell phones) and called him to come pick me up. Don't ask me how I got a ride on a bus with a group of young college men going to a baseball game. I have no memory of the how, only the what. I was a friendly, sweet, but-make-no-mistake unstoppable force when I wanted to get my way. And that's how I showed up unexpectedly to surprise Mike. Unannounced. Uninhibited. Undeterred. Impulse fully ignited.

In my life, I've been known to act a time or two (or a few hundred) on impulse. Impulse once found a piece of gum stuck to Mike's stomach hair, which he still tells the story with feigned disgust. Impulse found me bringing a six-month old puppy home to our family of six without asking him. There would be no feigning Mike's disgust on this occasion. He was angry that I made a "fifteen-year commitment without him." It took him three days to get over my indulgent wrongdoing. He tried for a few days not to look at *our* new puppy, Ginger. Ginger and I eventually won him over…well, I won him over. Ginger would forever remain "Sheri's dog." Impulse has gotten me into a lot of trouble over the years, but it's also done its good. It isn't shy about helping others. It reacts. It offers. It speaks. It moves. It does.

I've always been an instinctual decision-maker. My impulsive nature has been appropriately dampened with age and wisdom, *and* because I'd like to keep my marriage intact. Impulse is not all bad, but like all feelings, it needs to have an advisor, someone to answer to. It can't just go running amuck every time it feels the urge to do something. Whether the triggered impulse is desire, sadness, pride, shame, anger, happiness, comfort, excitement, or whatever, there must be a rightly guided filter, something to set proper standards of right and wrong behavior.

That leads to some pertinent questions. What is right and wrong? Good and bad? If you listen to social commentary of any kind, you'll get a different answer. The world is vying for our attention of right and wrong. TV. News. Social Media. Sports. Family. Friends. Our churches and our pastors. And me. If you listen or watch or read *anything*, it has the propensity to capture your attention and draw you in. Some things are good. Some things are not-so-good, and others appear relatively benign, but honestly, how do you know?

How do we bring our feelings under the authority and will of God? How do we deny them? What does this look like? Doesn't God give us free will? How does the sovereignty of God come into play? What if our feelings are there, but stay hidden and we never act out on them? What about Repentance? Redemption? Freedom? Legalism? Grace?

Lions, tigers, and bears, oh my.

## I DON'T WANNA

I can't answer all these questions succinctly, nor do I want to. I can't give you a perfect solution, a program, or stop the evil and wickedness in your path. I just don't want any of us to be a foregone conclusion that we have no power to change that which we are called to change.

Paul says in his letter to the Romans, "I **do** not understand what I **do**. For what I want to **do**, I **do** not **do**, but what I hate, I **do**. (Rom. 7:15, emphasis added). Read the rest of Romans 7:15–20. You'll find twenty-three instances where Paul uses "do" or "does." Paul is, in essence, talking about his feelings and his desire to do what God says over and above the feelings which threaten to rule him. Paul says right afterwards, in verse 21, "Evil is right there with me." What a punch in the gut statement that is. Evil is right there with us. It's not going away, and neither is our propensity to follow, justify, and act on the self-elevating expression of our feelings.

Each day's choices are being filtered through how we feel. Just this morning, I fought the urge to throw in the towel and skip my morning walk. It was cold, drizzling, and unpleasant by anyone's standard. No one was making me walk. As the time ticked away, I wasn't sure who was going to win the battle, my *desire* for cozy warmth and comfort or my healthy morning *habit* of exercise. It was clear on this particular morning, "I didn't wanna." In order to accomplish the walk, I was going to have to overcome my lack of desire to do what I didn't want to do. Why? Because there was a higher purpose in the doing. Walking is good for my health, and it's also where I do the majority of my writing. There's nothing like walking to get my creative juices flowing.

I'm not going to tell you whether I took my walk or not, because that's not the point. The point is the battle itself. "I don't wanna," or in other cases depending on the circumstances, "I wanna," are choices every day, all day, infringing on our will as our desires and feelings take center stage. We are well trained to take the path of least resistance. Actually, it doesn't take much training. We are creatures born to least resistance. Young minds learn early that they don't feel like picking up their toys or taking a bath, and young minds turn into adolescent minds who don't feel like doing chores or homework or helping their parents (or even being nice). By the time we are adults, our instinct towards the path of least resistance is well established, as seen quite clearly in my opposition to take a rainy morning walk because it would make me uncomfortable, even as it was good for me.

Our lives are filled with choices of what we do and don't want to do. We don't feel like walking. We don't feel like reading the Bible. We don't feel like being patient. Or on the flip side, we feel like being lazy. We feel like eating a large ice cream cone. We feel like spending hours on social media. We feel like watching a not-so-good show on TV. Our feelings rule the place of decision-making more often than we realize.

I don't wanna…I do wanna…I feel like…I don't feel like…

You could take an index card of these four statements and fill in the blanks all day long. You'd start to become aware of how many things challenge how and what you feel like doing or not doing, and how you respond.

## RULING THE "WANNA"

I have to control the pull of what I want to be doing versus what I should be doing. We all do. There's nothing new in this. It's as old as Adam and Eve and the serpent in the garden who convinced them to rebel against the directive of God (to not eat from the tree of the knowledge of good and evil. Gen. 2:17). "I want what I want" is as old as the fall of man.  It was the same with Cain, the firstborn son of Adam and Eve, when God corrects his wicked heart and tells him, "Sin is crouching at your door; it desires to have you, but you must rule over it" (Gen. 4:7).

We must overcome the wickedness in us leading to a path of destruction, and like my old impulsive self, filter *I wanna, I don't wanna. I feel like,* and *I don't feel like* through God's Word, and not our feelings of the moment.

How can our feelings, created *and* intended for us *also* be adversarial to our goodness and holiness? How do we balance the great gift of feelings with the necessary task to restrain and/or defeat them in order to live godly lives? There are so many questions as I consider the part of us that is our feelings, and it's not an easy construct. I won't get it right. I'm no theologian or psychiatrist, even as I am hoping to plant a seed of consideration on how we view our feelings, and prompt each of us to search God's Word on the matter.

## A FEELING GOD

Is God anti-feeling? Genesis 1:27 says we are "created in God's image," so certainly part of that image has to do with our emotions. God himself has them, and you'll find references to God's emotions throughout the Old Testament, as well as the emotions of Jesus as witnessed in the New Testament.

Consider these verses taken randomly from Scripture to make this point:

> Genesis 6:6, "The LORD regretted. His heart was deeply troubled.

> Deuteronomy 4:24, "The LORD your God is a devouring fire; he is a jealous God,"

> or 4:31, "God is a merciful God,"

> and 4:37, "God loved your ancestors."

> Deuteronomy 10:15, "The LORD set his affection… and loved them."

> In Isaiah 54:7–8, we see God's anger, kindness, and compassion.

> In Job 42:7, God says, "I am angry."

> Isaiah 51:1, "You have drunk the from the cup of the LORD's wrath."

> Matthew 17:5, "This is my Son, whom I love; with him I am well pleased."

Jesus, as seen throughout the four Gospels, showed anger, fatigue, forgiveness, and compassion. He also criticized, rebuked, showed amazement, kindness, sternness, love, and delight, and in the shortest verse in the Bible, we see "Jesus wept" (John 11:35). On the eve of his arrest, it tells us in Matthew 26:38, Jesus was "sorrowful and troubled, overwhelmed with sorrow to the point of death." On the cross Jesus cries out, "My God, my God, why have you forsaken me?" (Matt. 27:46). Pain. Sorrow. Suffering. Loss. Jesus is our great witness to the beauty and depth and validity of emotions as seen in the character of God. The Holy Spirit as triune God is seen grieving our sin (Eph. 4:30).

We clearly see emotions in the character of the triune God throughout the Old and New Testament. To deny our emotions would be to deny what God has created within each of us, and I'm not suggesting this. We are not to be void of the gift of our emotions even as we are to appropriate them to God's authority.

## SO THAT IT WILL GO WELL FOR YOU

Jesus said, "You must deny yourself if you want to be my disciple" (Matt. 16:24…emphasis added). Jesus also said, "Whoever has my commands and keeps them is the one who loves me. The one who loves me will be loved by my Father, and I too will love them and show myself to them" (John 14:21). This comes on the heels of Jesus promising the disciples that he will give [another] advocate (along with Jesus), the "Spirit of truth, the one who will live and be in you" (John 14:15–17). Who is the one who loves Jesus? The one who keeps his commands. He says we love him if we *do something*.

Once we become more equipped to slay our feelings by being obedient to the Word and *do*ing what God calls us to *do*, the "I wanna" or "I don't wanna" start to weaken their hold on our hearts and our lives. We rightly position ourselves to be a servant of Jesus, rather than a servant of our always-fighting-to-be-first feelings.

The world will tell you feelings are valid, whatever they are. Conversely, the Word tells you, "The heart is deceitful" (Jer. 17:9), and if you "walk by the Spirit, you will not walk by your feelings (flesh), and your feelings (flesh) desire what is contrary to the Spirit, and the Spirit what is contrary to your feelings (flesh). They are in conflict with each other, so that you are not to do whatever you want" (Gal. 5:16–17). Why do we want to consider this important? Why do we want to demote our feelings to their proper position?

*So that it will go well for you.* Don't we want it to go well for us? Isn't the denial of impulses, desires, and behaviors which are contrary to God's Word worth it in the end? They are, and once we recognize our feelings don't have our best interests at heart, our life will change accordingly. I'm not talking to those who don't know Jesus. They aren't going to hear this message well. I'm talking to those of us who follow Jesus and believe restraint and denial, like parents' training us when we are young, is God's way to train us to have a good and holy life, not one devoid of problems, mind you, but one filled with joy. A life which ultimately has little to do with our circumstances (trust me, we'll get to that one), and everything to do with trust, obedience, and holy desires of our heart. Holy desires lead us to an abundant life, the kind of abundance God intends for us to have (not worldly abundance), and that kind of life is going to take you choosing God over you choosing you.

And while this whole idea of bringing our feelings under the rulership of God and his Word sounds stifling, it is a subjugated life that brings freedom from chaos. Freedom from impulse. Freedom from sin. Freedom from being pulled to the right, or to the left or swayed by the happenings of the day, the happenings of circumstances, or the happenings of a culture vying for your attention. 2nd Peter 2:19 says, "People are slaves to whatever has mastered them."

Surrender is a beautiful place to be and if you're a believer, it's the only place to be. Surrendered to keep the commandments of God out of the overflow of an obedient *doing* heart, a heart transformed by a loving God who died to save us. This is the appropriate feeling in our lives. Love God with all your heart and love others. Let's be a slave to that idea.

## NO CONDEMNATION

"There is now no condemnation to those who are in Christ Jesus" (Rom. 8:1). Jesus died for our sins. He died for those unruly feelings. He is sovereign over them. He knows them before we do. And he is our Mediator, interceding at the right hand of God, along with the Spirit's work in our lives to correct, redirect, and guide us. What does it take to change? Humility. Meekness. Wisdom. Commitment. Trust. Obedience. None of which you can do on your own. All of which you can ask for and receive.

There is a progression of Paul's first letter to the Romans when he was younger, fighting the battle of "I wanna" and "I don't wanna" to when he is an old man writing his last letters. In 2nd Timothy 4:17–18, Paul writes (in part), "But the Lord stood at my side and gave me strength. I was delivered from the lion's mouth. The Lord will bring me safely to his heavenly kingdom." We see a more mature relinquishment of Paul. His old life is behind him, and his mature life is an example of a life sanctified and made holy to God. We are chosen to be saved and saved because we are chosen. It is not by our good works, not by our belief in God, or our ability or lack thereof to control our emotions. It's by God's will and grace any of us are saved or changed at all. The good works the Spirit continues in us are "excellent and profitable for everyone" (Titus 3:8), and we become changed because God has designed that change in us. The servant-hood we seek by knowing Jesus is the work of the Spirit, and simply our response to it, not our control of it. I know, there's nothing simple about it, and yet it's not complicated.

I fear I'm falling all over myself handling this topic of emotions, but it's really ok. I'm not the end-all. I'm only the *wanna-be* explorer, a faithful servant trying to find for myself a holy way of living. It'll be ok. I can trust God's sovereignty over my words and your heart. There's relief in knowing this.

So, let's get going. Let's explore some specific emotions together, as we consider how to draw from truth and seek God's best for us in our yearning to defeat our runaway emotions, the ones that work against a worthy and holy strong faith. Do not be afraid.

# CHAPTER 3

## Study and Reflection

Bible verse: *Galatians 5:17* – Read.
Write out in the space below:

_______________________________________________

_______________________________________________

_______________________________________________

_______________________________________________

*So that you are not to do whatever you want.* Whoa. That's such a powerful statement.

Continue to read on in Galatians and you find this; "Those who live like this will not inherit the kingdom of God" (Gal. 5:21). Live like what? Among the many ways listed (in Gal. 5:19-20) is "impurity, discord, and selfish ambition…and the like."

But it says in Gal. 5:25, "Since we live by the Spirit, let us keep in step with the Spirit.'"

We're going to discuss the Holy Spirit's role in our lives in Chapter 15, but for now, I want us to consider this idea that we can't do whatever we want, and we must keep in step with the Spirit.

Mike is 6'7" and you'd think that because his legs go on for miles, I'd have trouble keeping up with him when we walk together, but it's not like that. I'm the faster walker of the two of us (no pun intended). I'm always trying to adjust my gate to match his slower pace, and I've been known to get frustrated a time or two. In fact, I'm usually a good foot or two in front of him, as if walking ahead of him will urge him on. It never seems to work. He's got his pace, and I've got mine. To be honest, it takes adjusting *my* expectations and *my* feelings of impatience to calm my spirit, adjust my gate, and simply enjoy walking together.

Perhaps you find this a silly analogy, but when I think of walking with the Spirit and being in step with the Spirit, I think of adjusting my gate to slow down, listen, and be patient in the waiting. And not walk in frustration and/or disobedience. We are not meant to walk in our own pace. We aren't meant to go our own way. We are to keep in step and have joy in the keeping.

When I adjust my ways, I adjust my expectations (and my emotions) and when I do, I relax. Restraint and release bring me greater joy and I can be with God (in the same way I can be with Mike) and not worry so much about where I'm going and how fast I'll get there. The higher value is simply to be with Jesus and listen to the Spirit.

Do you live by the Spirit? What does that look like? How can you best keep in step with the Spirit?

What areas of your life do you need to adjust your gate and do less of what you want to do and more of what the Spirit is leading you to do? (work, home, quiet time, etc.)

As in most things, it's a matter of practice. We wait on God. Pray for guidance. Listen to the Holy Spirit by responding to good opportunities to serve and love. Walk in the truth of the Word. Humble ourselves. It's a matter of restraint, not a matter of "doing whatever we want to do." That's where we can relax and find the joy of the Lord.

> *Lord, we're not good at denying ourselves when it comes to much of anything…certainly not when it comes to acting on our feelings. We want what we want, and we want it now, but that's not your desire for our lives. We pray for patience in the waiting and that our "want" will not be greater than your "want." Thank you for reminding us that in the middle of pacing our steps to match yours, we'll find joy. Yet your will be done. Amen.*

# 4

# Fear: The Dreaded Awful

*The awful is out there just waiting to bring me down.*

The call startles me alert at nine pm. I pick up my phone and see Sarah's number, and an all-familiar knot of dread starts to form. She knows I'm usually asleep by now. Dread has been well trained in me and is often the first place I go. I answer the phone, hear my daughter crying, and for a second my breathing stops, long enough to prepare myself for the awful, whatever the awful might be. The awful is out there just waiting to bring me down.

Sarah weeps as she tells me a nurse (at the earlier five o'clock closing hour) mentioned meningitis as a possibility for her ongoing symptoms of neck soreness and fever. Turning to Google for answers, she's had four long hours to succumb to irrational fear. I've not heard her this scared before, and after all, she has a three-year-old daughter and a seven-month-old son. I calm her down and tell her she'll be fine. I assure her that if she really had deadly meningitis, she'd already be dead. I'm full of such sound advice on the edge of sleep. Nonetheless, it does the trick, and she calms down. We hang up. I Google meningitis and convince myself she'll be dead by morning.

It's not the first time I've killed off a family member. They are consistently coming to their demise in my imagination, more times than I'm willing to admit. A slip in the pool. A plane ride. A snowstorm, heavy rain, wind, or any kind of weather really. The common cold. If it can be imagined, I've probably imagined it. Mike had covid and went to the hospital and by the time I picked him up five hours later with an array of medications, I had planned his funeral, written a beautiful and touching obituary, considered my widowhood, and contemplated whether I would stay in the house or move. To those of you who don't deal with worry, you'll think I'm exaggerating. To those of you who are like me, you'll get it. You'll just know. It doesn't take much to incite *the awful* and plan out the rest of your life.

I invite worry into my life as easily as inviting a good friend over for lunch. I let it in, feed it, and entertain it, but unlike a friend, it doesn't leave at the appointed time. It hangs around longer than wanted, sometimes moving in and messing up my joy. It's not worry's fault. It's my resistance to let it go, because if I hang onto it, perhaps I'll have some semblance of control. I don't. I know this logically, yet worry still hangs around because the ones I love fiercely are the ones I don't want to lose.

## THE CAMP OF DREAD

Ecclesiastes 7:4 says, "A wise person thinks a lot about death" (NLT), so while I am, according to Scripture, a wise person, I have to be on guard to not overindulge this part of my thought life. I think there are two camps of people. The worriers and the non-worriers. Mike is a non-worrier. Recently, I asked him if he thought about death as often as I do, and he looked at me as if he hasn't known me for over forty years. I thought everyone thinks about death as much as I do. It helps to be in a relationship where at least one of you is a non-worrier. Put two worriers together and I'd be worried about that. You can't both walk around thinking about death all day.

Do you know which camp you're in? Do you dread the awful, trying to predict and control which corner it's around? Or are you like Mike, taking life in stride, calm and relatively worry-free unless there's something to worry about? And even then, you don't get too far ahead of yourself. If you're the latter, I wish I were more like you. I'm working on it. Truly I am.

So, did Sarah have meningitis? No, she didn't. She discovered the nurse incorrectly read her file of having a high white blood cell count, which she had seven months prior, a normal symptom of giving birth (but also a symptom of meningitis).

A couple of months after this incident, Sarah called into the same doctor's office dealing with double vision. This time they mention the possibility of Multiple Sclerosis (Personally, I think she should switch doctors but that's a rant for another day). You'd think she'd have learned her lesson, but she didn't. She's her mother's daughter after all. Sarah googles MS and reads a few lines which mention *seven years*. She stops reading and breaks down crying with worry. Sister Jess sweeps in for the cleanup, straightens Sarah out, telling her she doesn't have seven years to live, but instead, a life expectancy seven years less than normal. They nervously joke that Jess will die at one hundred and Sarah will die at ninety-three.

## FEAR IS OPPORTUNITY TO TRUST

We sometimes trivialize our anxieties, yet fear is not a trivial matter. The anxieties of worry are real. Fears are enhanced by our experiences. Anyone who has been on this earth for an extended period of time has most likely experienced trauma, loss, sorrow, and pain. We know too much. We are no longer innocent. Fear is exacerbated by our history of difficult experiences and our knowledge of tragedies within a much-too-small world.

I didn't use to worry as much in my younger years as I have in these later years. I've experienced two emergency C-sections, four miscarriages, flown twice to Russia to adopt two daughters (which can give anyone anxiety), tried to fix the depth of their trauma, saw most of the women in my family deal with the devastation of breast cancer, and watched my mother die a cruel slow death from breast cancer at age fifty-seven. I was partially paralyzed for months with a brain tumor as I faced possible disability and/or death. I watched Mike herniate a disc in his back and have surgery. I shared in the heartbreak of a daughter's miscarriage, and experienced illnesses and deaths within my circle of friends and family. Mike and I have been part of a human trafficking rescue ministry and don't get me started on that slippery slope of reality (and imagination). There's non-stop exposure to the news, if you're inclined to read or watch it (I am not). We know things we wish we didn't. It's hard to not go through life without some sort of PTSD reactivity of life's cumulative experiences ready to set our fear-meter off at a moment's notice. We are well-educated on the fragility of life. I try not to fear the future, but I don't always succeed. I know the kind of pain that can enter when you're least expecting it.

## NO SHAME IN FEAR

God knows every thought we have, so we don't have to pretend our fears don't exist. God exhorts us to trust him and not fear yet treats fear tenderly and often throughout the Bible. Jesus tells us in Matthew 10:31, "So don't be afraid; you are worth more than many sparrows." Jesus speaks often to people's fears because he meets us where we're at, knows how real our fears are, and continually guides us to trust the Father. Fear can be an inroad to grow in our belief and trust of the Lord.

Resist telling someone they're sinning because of their fear. That's harsh and shaming, and not the way Jesus treated those he cared about. Shaming someone only stops them from being vulnerable enough to admit their fears. It doesn't stop them from experiencing fear. We want to be able to give permission and compassion to others in all things.

Fear is to be respected as a gift and guidance from God. Fear warns us. Once, when I lived in the country where neighbors were spread out, I answered the door to a man who instantly scared me. My fear radar shot way up. Fortunately, our dog felt it too as she growled and snarled the man all the way back down our very long driveway, something she'd never done before or after. Fear is a God-given emotion appropriately warning us (and our dog Riley) away from trouble.

While we are to treat fear with compassion, our decisions about fear (and yes, they can be decisions) can lead us into sin. Fear is often wasted energy in its purposelessness. I'm reminded how often my fears have not been realized and how they have sapped my joy or led to sleepless nights (like the one I convinced myself Sarah would not make it through).

My mom died at fifty-seven. Her mom died at fifty-seven. How often was I scared that I too would die at fifty-seven? I don't want to say. Fear convinces us we'll somehow be guarded against tragedy, but trust me, it's *never* the expected, and *always* the unexpected which catches us off guard, like a brain tumor when you're expecting breast cancer.

## IMAGINED FEARS ARE REAL

Fears are practiced and rehearsed and the more we rehearse them, the better we become at inciting them at a moment's notice. I work to trust God more and not rehearse every fearful thought that pops in my head. I draw on the knowledge that God loves me "with an everlasting love" (Jer. 31:3) to combat my fears. A loving God, who knows every hair on my head, who is sovereign and omnipotent over all things, is not one who is waiting to catch me or my family unaware and devastate our lives. He wants to *strengthen* and *uphold* (Isaiah 41:10). He wants our trust and that means setting fears and desire for self-protection aside.

While fear is not in itself a sin, it is sinful to indulge in the feeling of it and respond in a manner that leads us away from God. We want to be cautioned to not court or indulge our feelings over and above trusting in God. The goal of our lives is not about safety and protection. It's not even about our families (try telling my thoughts this). The goal is God. Simply. Purely. Always.

Our imagination is not our destiny. Our thoughts aren't truth, yet they often rewire us as if they are. How often do we fear something which hasn't and never will happen? I read a sad story of a child killed by a brick falling from a high-rise building when the child was with his grandmother. A grandparent's worst nightmare is that something bad will happen on their watch. In a million years, the brick scenario couldn't have been imagined or foreseen. We try to predict, yet we can't. It's like the cancer I never got, or the predicted age I was scared I wouldn't make it past. I didn't admit my fears to anyone, but they were there, deep within me, working on me…working on me…working on me. The tumor helped me see that projecting my future is baseless. It showed me how fruitless my wasted worry of breast cancer was. It's never the expected issues in our lives that throw us for a loop. It's *always* the unexpected.

## GUARD YOUR HEART AND SEEK THE LIGHT

Does it get easier as we age? I'm not sure it does. Loss and pain become more prevalent with age, and because they do, we must continue to stay on guard. I still work on releasing my fears, and I'm glad to admit as my faith grows, fear lessens its grip on me.

Proverbs 4:23 says, "Above all else, guard your heart, for everything you do flows from it." We need to guard our hearts from fear. We need to recognize how it holds us captive, and we must rely on the truths of God to turn our hearts away from fear and towards him. Psalm 27:1, "The LORD is my light and my salvation – whom shall I fear?"

The Lord is my light and my salvation, and because he is, I can persevere through my fears. Jesus will not let go of me. And he won't let go of you. He came to this earth to die for you and me. His promises can be trusted. If he commands us to *count it all joy* (James 1:2), then count it we must, because like a child trusting a parent, we can overcome the fears we fight against, threatening to unravel us at every turn. We can move forward knowing it's not our control that makes the difference but our release of control to the one who asks for it. God yearns for your heart and for your good. Let it be enough. It's enough for me…that is, when I'm not letting myself worry about the awful.

# CHAPTER 4

## Study and Reflection

Bible verse: All of *Isaiah 55* – Read.
Write out (the two lines that start with "listen"
as found in verses 2 and 3) in the space below:

___

Mike and I take a week each year to go to Florida to break up the cold gray winter. Each time we go, we choose a new destination, and this year was spent in Ft. Lauderdale. The rental car company didn't have the vehicle we reserved, and we ended up in a Ram pickup, a larger vehicle than we wanted. The downtown Ft. Lauderdale coast is dense with people and traffic, and parking wasn't always easy. Every time we traveled in and around the city, I was a nervous nellie, and because my nerves were getting the better of me, I started looking out the window at the sights, rather than be a backseat driver clinging to my door handle for dear life (don't judge me). Turning away did a pretty good job at removing most (not all) of my anxieties. Not looking was a good thing for me.

Why do we fear? In this particular case, it was because I lacked control over my safety. I think that's a pretty common theme for our anxieties and fears. The world is small. Every shooting, hurricane, accident, tragedy, and crisis is on full display the instant it happens. The media is driven by bad news, not good news. It's an overwhelmingly negative dangerous world out there if you are so inclined to tune in.

We look. We worry. We look some more. We worry some more. News. Social media. All trying desperately to capture our attention. All skewed to sensationalize. All designed to make us more afraid.

There are many places in the Bible that talk about what we set our minds on, and Isaiah 55 is among them. If you read all of Isaiah 55, you will find some instructions:

- Eat what is good.
- Give ear.
- Come to me.
- Listen, that you may live.
- Seek the Lord.
- Call on him.
- Turn to the Lord.

The verses in Isaiah tell us that God's Word will not return to us empty which implies that we should know God's Word. Isaiah 55 doesn't specifically address fear, but fear is among those things we incline our hearts to. We need to know and listen to the bread of life given in Christ, not the dread of life given in the world.

I'd like to challenge each of us to evaluate what we're putting into our hearts and minds by asking a few questions:

1. Is what I'm viewing (or reading) making me more afraid?
2. Is it bringing me to a place of more or less joy?
3. Is it filling me up with scriptural truths and more of God?
4. If not, is there something I can do now to change this?

Isaiah 55 is titled (in the NIV), *Invitation to the Thirsty*. If you are thirsty, God is inviting you to come to the waters of life. There's no good reason to saturate ourselves with the troubles of the world when all it will do is deplete us and make us angry and afraid. Turn to the Word and fill your tank up with that which is life-giving and spirit-building.

> *Lord, we turn our fears over to you. We seek the Spirit's help to direct our minds, our eyes, and our ears away from the troubles of the world and towards the hope of Jesus, and the truths of the Word. Yet your will be done. Amen.*

# 5

# Control: By God's Design

*Control is so underrated when your head is bolted to a table.*

It wasn't my first time in the tube. I'd already had numerous MRIs, but this time I'd be wearing a fitted mask with my head securely bolted to the imaging table. This time there'd be a gamma knife (which isn't a knife at all), invading my lemon-sized tumor, and I'd be in a constrictive tube for over an hour.

I arrived at six in the morning, and without my normal infusion of coffee, I was tired. I told myself I'd go back to sleep as soon as I was in the tube. By the time the procedure started, a couple of hours later, I was fully awake, adrenalin flowing, pulse racing, and my imagination engaging all the possibilities. Sleep wasn't one of them.

Getting me in the tube was easy as the technicians tightened the large bolts to the table and slid me in. Keeping me there wasn't. A few minutes in, I started fighting the urge to cough and was certain my bladder was filling up. Erratic thoughts filled my mind. What if the gamma knife didn't hit the right spot? What if there was a fire and everyone had to run out of the building? How many people were in the control booth? I started to worry less about radiation hitting the right spot than I did dying a slow burning death on a table in a tube. While prone to worry, I'm not prone to panic attacks, and it was bad timing that this was turning into my first. I prayed and asked God to help me get through it, but my future burning body was getting the best of me.

I didn't want to cause trouble, but I had this *thing* in my right hand that would make it all go away. That *thing* was my way back to control. So, there I was, holding the *thing*, a ball, much like the top of a rubber turkey baster, which when squeezed, would send a signal, and shut the machine down allowing me to take back control. I willed myself to both squeeze and not squeeze the ball. I tried to calm myself, pray, and relax. It was not to be, and before I knew it, my grip tightened. The machine went quiet. I felt the shame of failure as relief washed over me. "Are you ok?" someone asked through the speakers. Instead of screaming, "Get me out of here," I found myself apologizing and meekly asking if I could "please have a sip of water and a moment to collect myself?"

Control is so underrated when your head is bolted to a table and you're imagining the smell of smoke. They slid the tube out and unscrewed the bolts. I sat up and slowly…very slowly…sipped the water, pretending I needed it, wishing I could get off the table and never come back. I breathed in my freedom knowing I had no choice but to hand control back and start over. And so, I did, bolts and all.

## WE ALL WANT CONTROL

Control. Who doesn't want it? We want control of everything. Our money. Our privacy. The boundaries around our homes. The privacy within our homes. The color of our walls. The things we watch. The things we eat. If and when we take a shower. The control we desire is learned. It's cultural. It's our false sense of security, because if we have more of it, we think we'll be happy and safe, and our families will be happy and safe. Control is greedy. The more it has, the more it wants. And control, like anything threatening to overtake us, is a thief. It robs us of joy. It robs us of relationships. It robs us of our trust in God, a trust he asks for, and if we give it, will find us with more joy and more safety, not less.

I have struggled to give away control. I've blamed this on being a

Type A personality, or being first-born, or raised in a family of tough guys, and of course, the old "I am who I am" excuse. There are many excuses for wanting to control the world. Control is a value; one we hold tightly or loosely. I have always held it tightly, and it's only in my later years that it no longer rules my life. One of the great gifts of the tumor was being forced to relinquish control, and while scary, it taught me the value of giving my life over to the One who has it anyway.

## REWORKING GOD'S PLAN

Among the best examples of control in the Bible is found in the story of Sarai (before she was renamed Sarah). The Lord told Abram (before he was renamed Abraham) in Genesis 12:2, "I will make you into a great nation, and I will bless you; I will make your name great, and you will be a blessing." Abram and Sarai were seventy-five and sixty-five years old, respectively, when the Lord told Abram this (yes, they lived longer back then, but even for that time period, it was old to have a child). The years passed and still, there were no children for Sarai and Abram. Can you imagine their confusion? They must have wondered, "How is God going to make us into a great nation without children? What are we to do?"

Therein lies the first question we often ask ourselves: *What are we to do?* We don't trust God. We don't trust his provision. We don't trust his timing. We don't trust his love. We only trust ourselves.

In Genesis 16:2, Sarai says, "The LORD has kept me from having children." What a powerful statement. *The Lord has kept me from having children.* Aren't we sometimes the same? We, as believers, profess to trust God, yet we think God is keeping something good from us and doesn't have our best interests at heart. It's the same theme of Adam and Eve in the garden. The serpent convinced them to eat from the tree of life, the only tree God prohibited, proclaiming they "would be like God." Adam and Eve disobeyed God thinking he was keeping something good from them.

Sarai, not trusting God, instructed Abram to sleep with her slave, Hagar, and "build a family." She and Abram used someone else in order to get the child they wanted and expected. They selfishly re-worked an outcome according to their plans and their timetable, hurting others in the process, including themselves.

We want what we want, and nothing is going to stop us. I have to admit, this had been a theme of my strong willed, controlling young-er self. I thought I knew what was best for me, or simply, I wanted what I wanted. We are good at reworking outcomes, and consequent-ly, we are good at messing things up. We are a people patterned in go-ing our own way, but patterned disobedience leads to consequences.

## CONSEQUENCES OF A REWORKED PLAN

Sarai forced a child within her family. She was old and impatient, and didn't trust what God told Abram, not without her interven-tion. Certainly, she had aged beyond normal child-bearing age, and perhaps started to reinterpret what God *actually* meant. It could've been she imagined God wanted her to use Hagar to gain the family he promised. Sarai, like many of us, reworked God's plan to fit the plan she desired. It's easy to manipulate and conjure up the plan we want. We're good at seeing a road God doesn't put in front of us. "*Just do it*" wasn't just a marketing campaign, it's often our life's credence. My own life's theology, as discussed in my previous book, *Strong*, was "where there's a will, there's a way." I have been guilty of making my own way, thinking my will was powerful enough to get whatever it was I wanted.

So, Sarai gives Hagar to a complicit Abram. Hagar becomes preg-nant and has a son (Ishmael). Sarai resents Hagar. Hagar resents Sarai. Abram seems to turn a deaf ear to the conflict. Sarai mistreats Hagar. Hagar runs away. Abuse. Conflict. Heartache. Misunderstanding. What an absolute mess.

Do you see the consequences of Sarai and Abram's disobedience? Genesis 15–18 is a fascinating read. I encourage you to read the whole story, and then continue on to when Sarai, renamed Sarah, finally *was* blessed with a son when she was ninety-years old, and Abram, renamed Abraham, was one-hundred-years old. God's plans were not thwarted, even as they did their best to mess it all up.

Proverbs 19:21 says, "Many are the plans in a person's heart, but it is the LORD's purpose that prevails." Sarah and Abraham ended up taking the more difficult route, yet that route didn't thwart the purposes of God. It just made it a lot more difficult and painful for Sarah and Abraham and everyone involved.

## A HEART CHANGE

When I experienced a complete lack of control in my life, I started to release more of it to God. I saw the wisdom of release, patience, restraint, and listening for the Spirit's guidance through reading Scripture and waiting for an answer. I started to want God's answer over my own and that changed everything for me. Patience and restraint used to be so frustrating. Now they are a lifeline and a blessing. I know if it's within God's will, he'll bring it to fruition, and if it's not, it won't happen. If it's not within God's will, I don't want it. That's been a game-changer for me. I no longer want what isn't in God's will for my life. This change in mind and heart is what takes away frustration, disappointment, "me" expectations, and distractions in life. I have learned that God's way is always the right and better way.

## GOD LOVES AND BLESSES *OUR* WAY

Does this mean God will leave us and not bless or love us if we choose our own way? Absolutely not. While there *will* be consequences, we aren't doomed because we chose our own way. God loves us infinitely, and because he does, he can use any road we are on for our good and his glory. His promises still stand: "God knows every hair on your head," "God's plan is to prosper you, and give you a hope and a future," "Do not be afraid. I am your shield, your very great reward," (Luke 12:7, Jer. 29:11, Gen. 15:1, respectively…paraphrased).

God meets us where we're at, even in our disobedience. He doesn't give up on us. 2nd Peter 3:9 says, "God is patient with you, not wanting anyone to perish, but everyone to come to repentance." The grace Jesus gave at the cross is greater than our disobedience, even while we *will* face the consequences of our disobedience. God didn't leave

Sarah and Abraham. He kept his promises to them. Our way doesn't drive God away.

## WE HAVE TO TRUST

Bolted to a table in a tube, relying on the expertise of others to radiate the proper location in my brain, was an extreme exercise in trust and release. When it was time to be re-bolted to the table and slide back in, I still had the squeeze ball in my hand, but I had to restrain myself. I had to let go and I did, successfully completing the radiation treatment. I've done numerous MRIs and procedures on my brain, but none as harrowing as that gamma knife radiation treatment. I had to trust in the hand guiding the laser, and let's face it, there could have been an error. There could have been adverse side effects (there were some). Life is full of decisions that lead to a range of favorable and unfavorable outcomes.

The control we hand over to God is about trust. We're relying on the expertise of God and he's God, after all. He's trustworthy. The outcome is already promised. It's eternal. We have everything to gain by trusting and releasing our lives to God. We have everything to gain by remembering God loves us and wants our best. We have to trust in his love.

Therein lies a core statement and commitment in our walk with God. We have to trust. We have to let go of the control we think we have. It's a daily commitment. God is asking for the control, not because he doesn't already have it, but because it's good for us to recognize our need to hand it over to him (and not make a mess of things). Proverbs 3:5–6 says, "Trust in the LORD with all your heart and lean not on your own understanding; in all your ways submit to him, and he will make your paths straight." He will make your paths straight. In all your ways. You can trust him.

# CHAPTER 5

## Study and Reflection

Bible verse: *Matthew 8:23-27* – Read.
Write out *v. 27* in the space below:

_______________________________________________

_______________________________________________

_______________________________________________

_______________________________________________

Fear and control are almost always intertwined. They go together like lightning and thunder. In fact, you could search for Bible passages on both and come up with the same passages. The control I used to seek, knowingly and unknowingly, was always based in fear of something. Fear of uncertainty, unpredictability, and/or failure.

Matthew 8:23-27 is a good example of feeling out of control.

List any words or phrases which show that these verses in Matthew are about fear:

_______________________________________________

_______________________________________________

_______________________________________________

The words or phrases I came up with were these five:

- Furious storm.
- Waves swept over the boat.
- Lord, save us!

- We're going to drown!
- Why are you so afraid?

I don't think there are any of us who would not have reacted the way the disciples did. Their fear seems completely reasonable, even warranted, and yet…Jesus is rather harsh on them. What did he call their faith?

The disciples clearly *felt* out of control (because they were). Jesus clearly was *in* control.

Can you think of an instance when you felt completely out of control like the disciples (or my gamma knife radiation)?

What are some descriptive words you'd use to describe those circumstances and your feelings?

You might have said angry, scared, confused, annoyed, disoriented, and sometimes, even panicked. There are a host of emotions that come with feeling out of control, all proportionate to the circumstance.

Our text tells us Jesus rebuked (or silenced) the winds and the waves, and the result was "a great calm."

A great calm.  Being out of control is scary, and yet Jesus makes it clear in this passage that he is our great calm, as we are called to trust him.

These verses are a reminder to not let control get the better of us. We can practice letting Jesus take the helm of our fears and our propensity to want to control everything around us. We can let him take over because we *can* trust him, even in the storms of life.

> *Lord, whether we try to control because we are afraid*
> *or whether we control because we are selfish, all is a*
> *turning away from you. Help us affix our hearts and*
> *minds to walking in the strength and patience and*
> *confidence that you are there to calm the storms and*
> *silence the chaos around us. Yet your will be done.*
> *Amen.*

# 6

## Shame: A Call Unanswered

*There, in the deafening silence I felt like
I had committed a huge parenting sin.*

I have a tribe, a beloved group of women who are my best friends
and have been so for more than twenty-five years. We've laughed and
cried together as we've shared in the intimate moments of our lives.
They know me best, and so it's unexpected that one of my greatest
incidents of remembered shame comes from within this group, more
than fifteen years ago. It came on the heels of a simple statement I
made, and I'd be willing to bet none of my friends remembers it.
Shame is not always recognized by the giver, even as it burns in the
memory of the receiver.

There we were one Bible study morning, a chatty group of women
talking over each other the way women more-than-sometimes do,
loving our coffee and pastries as much as we loved the study itself.
I spoke without hesitation. I was in a safe space. I would argue it's
worse when you have no anticipation of shame's arrival. It slaps you
in the face when you're least expecting it.

"After I bathe the girls at night, I dress them in their jeans for
school the next morning, so all I have to do is wake them, feed them,
and put them in the car," I said with a knowing grin. The laughter

halted. The room quieted. No one responded. Not one word was spoken. Shame entered in.

At the time, our youngest daughters were seven and eight, and the statement came with the discussion of how difficult mornings were for each of us moms. In those days, Mike and I had strategies for everything we did, and we used any technique necessary to make life manageable from the opposition that surrounded us. Everything we did was built around a plan. Dressing our daughters in jeans in preparation for the next morning was part of that plan, and to us, was *nothing*.

I said it light-heartedly, expecting laughter, but in the deafening silence, I felt like I had committed a huge parenting sin. The silence didn't resolve. No one lightened my load, and while it seemed to last forever, the group quickly moved on to someone else, and my bad parenting was soon forgotten. Except by me.

If dressing my children in jeans was bad enough to incur awkward silence from my closest friends, how could I tell them what was really going on behind closed doors? Could I reveal that I held down one of my daughters as she had what I described as a psychotic episode, scaring me with how out of control she was? Over the years, we had thousands of shocking moments that paled in comparison to wearing jeans to bed.

## BIRDS OF A FEATHER

That moment in time is among hundreds when I felt the expected *and* unexpected call of shame. How often do we find ourselves at the end of shame's call when we're least expecting it, and if we do, what do we remember? We remember how we felt. I'll never forget how I felt in that moment with my friends. I'll never forget how I felt when a first-grade teacher in a Christian classroom told me a parent complained because she felt cheated that her daughter had to be in the same classroom as mine. I'll never forget how I felt when, in desperation, I called the police and after arriving, one of them flippantly remarked, "All normal teenagers are sometimes disrespectful to their parents."

Shame showed up early in our adoption. It showed itself imme-diately when one of our daughters writhed and screamed for hours on the floor of the airplane traveling home from Russia to the U.S. We had given her ice cream which her little body wasn't accustomed to. It showed its ugly head again a couple weeks later, when our one-year-old, who had a terrible parasite called giardia, had diarrhea in a friend's baby pool. She was not at fault, of course, but I felt bad as I watched the host dump the water out, clean the pool, and put it away without hiding his disgust. I changed the gnat-infested smelly diaper in the grass nearby, trying to hide my tears. I wasn't to know in those early days how often shame would accompany our journey.

Shame enters all of our lives, some more than others. We don't feel good enough. What about you? Fill in the blank for yourself; I'll never forget how I felt when…

There was something important I learned that day with my friends in the Bible study. It's difficult to have true empathy for an-other when you aren't walking in their shoes. Twelve years into our journey with the girls, Mike and I went to our first therapeutic RAD (Reactive Attachment Disorder) training weekend with dozens of other parents and their children. It was remarkable. No matter how loud or threatening the kids were, no one batted an eye. There was not a shred of surprise or shame among the parents. We all became instant friends, our relatability like a warm blanket of knowing and understanding. Dressing children in jeans the night before school? This group of parents would have thought it genius.

Mike and I learned the only birds who could truly understand were the ones who were wearing the same feathers, so we started to seek our flock, and we became flock mentors. We wanted to ease the pain of others, knowing what it feels like to be an outcast, mis-understood, and embarrassed. We learned by our experiences to be empathetic listeners.

We've listened to struggling parents for hours on end, listened until we were worn out from both the listening and the trauma it reignited in us. Mike and I sometimes wondered if we'd done any good, until we reminded ourselves that letting others pour out their stories and their pain without judgment was the best "therapy" we could offer.

Over the years, Mike and I have heard the cries of the shamed:

*I love her. I hate her. Only you can understand.*

*You are one of the only people we share with and count on.*

*Both of my teenage daughters tried to commit suicide, and I was told to connect with you since you have problems too.*

*I'm afraid for my life. I found my daughter hiding knives in her bedroom drawer.*

*My son tried to kill himself the day before Mother's Day.*

*My ex-husband is going off the deep end. He sleeps with a gun under his pillow.*

*We had a rough rage episode and ended up in the ER. Some days we can't do this.*

*I'm struggling with my adopted son, and I don't like him right now. I've never admitted this to anyone before.*

*We're so lost. What would we do if others found out about our situation?*

The last statement surmises the core of shame. *What would we do if others found out about our situation?* Isn't that hitting the nail on the head? Isn't that the soul of shame's damage?

One of the best things I did in our journey with our adopted daughters was start a private blog. I invited close friends and family and actively shared for six years. It became a lifeline for Mike and me. Sharing helped us be transparent. Sharing gave us encouragement and confidence in our situation. Sharing led others to Mike's and my doorstep for advice. We became encouragers ourselves, helping others be brave in their own difficulties, often steering parents to get the help they needed.

What about you? What would you do if others found out about

your situation? There are many things you can do starting with seeking the right flock, those who will empathize and not criticize, who will lean into the truths of Scripture as they offer a soft, discerning, and caring ear. Sometimes that's the best others can offer, a listening ear and a soft heart. Before you know it, you'll be the one doing the listening to someone who needs it. There's something else you must do, and it might be the best, worthiest challenge I can give to you.

## REJECTING THE REJECTION

A few years ago, I gathered a dozen middle-aged mothers, most of whom had raised behaviorally challenged children. I asked if they could go back and give their younger selves one piece of advice, what would it be? The overwhelming response?

*Worry less about what others think.*

The moms said they would worry less. They didn't say they would try to change the minds of others, or they would say less, or even be silent. They would worry less. It's our worry we need to change, not the opinions of others. As a noun, shame is "a painful feeling of humiliation." As a verb, it is "someone making someone feel ashamed or humiliated." Both noun and verb are about how we feel and/or how we make others feel. Shame starts in the eye of the beholder (the giver) but is not obligated to be in the eye of the beholden (the intended receiver). In other words, we don't have to take what is being offered. We can make it less about us and more about the one who gives it.

Shame is based in rejection and while your opinions, ideas, and decisions might be rejected, you don't have to accept the rejection. Mike and I faced rejection when we decided to homeschool in 1998, when homeschooling wasn't widely known or accepted. We were strong in our decision, and while we wanted the blessings of others, we weren't deterred by not having them. They weren't rejecting us, per say, but rejecting our decision to homeschool, thinking it foolish. We were able to reject the rejection. That's not always easy to do, especially if you aren't confident in your decisions.

What we receive from others can take our emotions up and down. We are brought low when some are shocked because you dress your children in jeans before going to bed or brought high when someone else applauds you for the efficiency of it. The circumstance is the same yet how it is perceived is not. It's the up/down difference of those who raise an eyebrow when your child is screaming at you, or another who offers humor and their phone number because they've been in your shoes. It's the difference between a school who berates you for your unruly child, or one who caringly understands and helps you through it. In each of these, the circumstances are the same, the responses are not.

I determined a long time ago that I didn't have to be bound to the opinions of others, and over the years, I have felt less shame because I knew the truth of my life. I knew God ruled my life, and he is the one I found worth in.

## SHAME'S CLOSE PARTNER

There is a caveat, however, and it's the propensity for pride to enter in. The distance between shame and pride is a short one. Sharing my story started to elevate me. People reached out to Mike and me more frequently. They wanted our advice. They wanted our acceptance. I can't tell you how many times others reached out to us because, "You have problems too," or "Your life is a mess like mine." A messy life is attractive to others, because others want the strength you portray and the solutions you've found, and I've had to be careful I didn't lean too much on the pride of our situation. I didn't want to hang my hat on our hardships like a badge of honor (which I admittedly have done at times).

Applause isn't far away for those of us who wear suffering on our sleeve. I believe there is purpose in our pain, yet we should be cautioned that a godly purpose doesn't get overridden by pride in our pain. Our purpose, if used for right reasons, is meant to be used to care for others, and elevate Christ, not elevate ourselves.

Applause and shame are both initiated by a beholder, even as they are on opposite ends of the spectrum and can equally distract us from truth. Satan will use any tool to thwart truth in our lives, and we need to be cautioned accordingly. You, as the beholden, are to respond to both in the same way, whether you are shamed or lauded. Seek God and his truths and shun both as something others are attempting to give to you, not something you have to accept. Pride and shame are both deceivers and not from God.

God gives Scripture to guide us in right, wrong, and approved. 2 Timothy 2:15 says, "Do your best to present yourself to God as one approved, a worker who does not need to be ashamed and who correctly handles the word of truth."

Imagine if we could teach this principle to our children. While we can't protect them from bullying or keep them from the slippery slope of evil, can we better protect them from the priority they place on the opinions of others? Can we give them the Word as foundational and more significant than what they receive from the world? I believe we can, but it starts with us. It starts with what we believe, how we practice our beliefs, and how we live out those beliefs. Our lives are caught by our children (and others), not taught.

## THE HIGHER CALL OF GRACE

We can't force others to be compassionate or empathetic. We must practice giving grace. Giving grace is making allowances for another and it is our mandate to practice. We are tasked to give grace because we are tasked to forgive. "If one has a complaint against another, forgive them as the Lord forgave you" (Colossians 3:13…emphasis added).

What about my friends whose silence spoke volumes that day? They are still my best friends. Their silence didn't squelch my love for them, even though it hurt in the moment. I moved quickly past the hurt and in grace, knew they didn't understand how hard life was for us, nor did they intend to hurt me. What about the hundreds of underhanded, hurtful comments, judgments, and direct hits I took over the years because of our struggles? I've learned how to give grace many times over because if I didn't, I'd live in bitterness, self-righteousness, defensiveness, and be a slave to my feelings.

We want to "have our minds set on what the Spirit desires" (Rom.

8:5), and not be "governed by the flesh" (v. 6). We, in the "flesh cannot please God" (v. 8). Shame is of the flesh. Pride is of the flesh.

I don't mean to sound trite here. I don't mean to come across like this is easy. It's not. There's a reason I remember the deafening silence of my Bible study group all those years ago. Judgment hurts. I understand the hurt, and like anything worthy, this is for us to practice. The Spirit can guide us and help us through it. In the end, it's the practice of remembering who loves you and who you belong to that is the compass you must cling to. And while you may not rid yourself of all shame, you will greatly lessen its impact and control on your life.

## UNASHAMED OF THE GOSPEL

The root of shame goes deep into every crevice of our lives, and our avoidance of it may be the biggest single reason we don't share the good news of the Gospel. I avoid the possibility of rejection rather than letting the Spirit be bold through me. Romans 1:16 says, "For I am not ashamed of the gospel, because it is the power of God that brings salvation to everyone who believes." It's easier to write my faith down through words in a book, than it is to tell it to someone's face. I am so often a coward. Yet, even in this, there is no shame. God is continually working on me. I practice truth, trust, and strength. I practice knowing the Word, trusting in God to use his Word in my life and the life of others, and choosing to be strong enough not to cave to shame's call on my life.

Jesus loves you. This I know. For the Bible tells me so. Jesus died on the cross for your sins and you are no longer condemned. Practice not *feeling* condemned. Seek Jesus. Know the Word. Listen to the Spirit. Forgive others. Forgive yourself. Now move on.

# CHAPTER 6

## Study and Reflection

Bible verse: *Mark 14:66–72* – Read.
Write out verse 68 in the space below:

_______________________________________________

_______________________________________________

_______________________________________________

_______________________________________________

Peter denied knowing Jesus to a lowly servant girl not long after he insisted emphatically to Jesus, "Even if I have to die with you, I will never disown you" (Mark 14:31). He must have felt incredible shame in that moment. When it was all said and done, and Peter's three denials came to pass, Peter "broke down and wept" (Mark 14:72). Matthew and Luke's Gospels say Peter wept bitterly. He was surely in distress and sorrow.

Shame is such a strong emotion, and a strong driver of how we respond. Yet, I don't want to focus on our response of shame which I have already addressed in this chapter. I want to focus on how Jesus sees us even in the midst of our shame.

Jesus predicted Peter's denial and yet, soon after that prediction, Jesus tells the disciples, "Do not let your hearts be troubled," and continues on to tell them, "I am going there [my Father's house] to prepare a place for you," and "I will come back and take you to be with me" (John 14:1-3…emphasis added).

Who else do you know who you can turn your back on, deny

knowing them, and they will love you anyway? And not just love you…love you deeply?

The thing to notice here is that despite the disciples' predicted rejection of Jesus, he doesn't turn his back on them. His compassion is no match for Peter's denials, or his shame, and it's no match for our sin. Jesus doesn't turn his back on us despite our unloveliness, our denial of him, and our shame in hiding who we are in Christ. He loves us through our shame.

Read Romans 8:38-39. Paraphrase below:

_______________________________________________

_______________________________________________

_______________________________________________

_______________________________________________

Our shame, our sin, nor anything else can separate us from the love of God that is in Christ Jesus our Lord.

We don't want to live in shame of who we are in Christ, but make no mistake about it, it's not what we do that we are to focus on, it's what Christ has already done for us. He loves us with an everlasting love and that we can count on…from here to eternity.

*Lord, it's not our shame we want to focus on getting rid of. It's remembering how much you love us, and knowing nothing will ever be able to separate us from that love which is in you, our Lord and Savior. Yet your will be done. Amen.*

7

# Anger: The Bitter End

*Bitterness is anger settled in for the ride,
festering until it's uglier than anger.*

If memory serves me well, this was the worst moment in my marriage. It was 1999, and Mike and I were set to go to his company's annual conference in Keystone, Colorado, and like most parents of young ones, we were looking forward to getting away just the two of us. The morning of our departure, Jess got a fever, and I stayed behind. Mike went as scheduled, not knowing whether I'd be able to join him, but by the end of the day, Jess's fever had disappeared. I flew out the next morning.

We had a lovely few days together at the conference, and as we checked back into the Denver Airport to fly home, we unexpectedly discovered that my one-day delay on the front end prompted a one-day delay on the back end. Since the flight was overbooked, there would be no chance of me getting on it. Mike offered to swap his ticket for mine, to which I said, "No, it's ok, you go."

Let me repeat. I said, *No, it's ok, you go.* These are the kinds of things you say which you don't mean, but you expect the other person to know you don't mean what you said. Ok, perhaps, this was really my issue, not Mike's.

In retrospect, twenty-five years later, I don't know why I refused his offer. It wasn't in my character to do so. If you read my first book, *Strong*, you might remember the huge fight Mike and I had (which I initiated) about being delayed one hour on our drive home from a North Carolina beach trip. A huge fight over one whole hour. While I promise I'm reformed now, I used to have heightened anxieties about getting home after being away. This trip to Colorado was no different, especially in light of having young children at home.

Mike offered one more time, and my answer was the same. He talked with the counter person who told him there would be numerous flights out, but as they were all booked, I'd have to wait on standby which meant there was no guarantee of when (or if) I'd get on a flight. I told him I'd be ok, and before I knew what hit me, he was walking onto the airplane. I was stunned. It was so out of character for him. I was *maybe-sort-of-ok* until the second he disappeared from my sight, still hoping he'd change his mind. I was sure he'd come to his senses, regain his honor, turn around and say, "I could never leave you behind. You go in my place." But no, he got on the plane. I watched it take off, and when the realization hit me that he was indeed gone, I started to cry. Normally a fairly self-sufficient individual, I became unglued at the idea of being stuck in the Denver Airport, but more than that, I was devastated he hadn't put my needs above his own. I continued crying until my cries turned into sobbing. I was crushed.

I composed myself long enough to approach the ticket counter, desperate to get onto the next flight, and throwing salt on my wounded heart, I was met with an outright nasty ticket counter worker. Her snippy attitude only increased my distress. I sat back down and cried some more. I didn't care what others around me thought. I was a red-faced blotchy pathetic crying mess.

Over the next couple of hours, my tears dried up, and I started to get angry. With each flight's departure without me on it, my anger grew. I was angry at Mike, and I was angry at God. In fact, I specifically remember telling God I was too angry to talk to him. I had no desire for God to speak into my heart. It felt good to be angry.

"People ruin their lives by their own foolishness, and then they are angry at the Lord" (Proverbs 19:3, NLT). This described me. I don't think I've ever been angrier at anyone than I was at Mike that day. It's the ones you love the most who can spear you the deepest. If you don't think bitterness can come quickly, let me tell you it can. I felt a bitterness rising in me which I had no desire to squelch.

I sat there for a few hours, watching each flight come and go until finally, I got on the fourth flight out. Relief to be on the plane, however, did nothing to dampen my bitterness. I was just getting started.

I had a layover in Chicago and when I entered the airport gate, there he was. Unbeknownst to me, Mike's flight had been delayed in Chicago (this was before we all had cell phones). By then, my anger had turned into full blown hate. He approached me cautiously, tail between his legs, and I treated him like he was nothing. He tried to talk to me. I ignored him and walked away as if I didn't know him. I reveled in my superior state of hate. I had no intention of forgiving him. I didn't want to be godly. I wanted to be a hater. The indulgence of my bitterness tasted good, and I had every right.

As was the hand of providence in all its craziness, Mike and I arrived in Harrisburg, our local airport, within ten minutes of each other. Ten minutes. We silently collected our bags, loaded up the car, and drove home together, he in his awful guilt, me in my lovely hate, both of us in complete silence.

We spent a couple of days hardly speaking. My heart was slowly softening with the normalcy of life and family, but I was still angry. On day three I received a card with a handwritten note from him:

> *I love you and I'm sorry. I got this card after we got back and have been trying to come up with the magic words since then. There aren't any. I wanted to make a list of reasons to justify why I did what I did. But those reasons don't matter. What matters is that I let you down and crushed your trust. I'm sorry. I wish we could go back and have it to do over again but we can't. I do want you to know that after I left, I prayed and agonized over leaving you.*

*I guess I already knew it wasn't the right decision. I prayed to God to take care of you and bring you home safely. Obviously, you are (and were) far better off in his wonderful hands than my selfish care. However, He has entrusted you to me and while I can't promise to be perfect, I do promise to try and do better. "Husbands, love your wives just as Christ loved the church and gave himself up for her." Ephesians 5:25. I'm sorry and I love you, Mike*

## THE COST OF THE CROSS

With Mike's heartfelt note and the two of us talking it out, forgiveness came, and with it a washing of my soul from any trace of the hate I had pledged my allegiance to. Something else came. A lesson. God spoke to my heart about where I was putting Mike in the hierarchy of my life. I was placing him on the highest pedestal. He had become the God of my life. God showed me Mike is capable of selfishness, and it opened my eyes to who the real Lord should be in my life. Mike has been my best friend and the kindest husband to me for more than forty years, but I learned the hard way that he's human, and he's not to be the God of my life. It's among the best faith lessons I've ever learned, and it set me on a different, holier path.

Ruth Bell Graham said it best when she said, "It is a foolish woman who expects her husband to be to her that which only Jesus Christ himself can be. Such expectations put a man under an impossible strain. The same goes for the man who expects too much from his wife."[2]

We expect much from those around us and they will disappoint us, no doubt. When we put our expectations on others, we diminish the cost of the cross, the one Jesus died on to redeem our sins. There was a great cost to Jesus on the cross and it's a cost we should hang onto for dear life.

What is the cost of the cross? It's for a husband who makes a self-

---

[2]  https://www.goodreads.com/quotes/101348-it-is-a-foolish-woman-who-expects-her-husband-to

ish decision. It's for a nasty ticket counter person. It's for my pride and hate, and every self-serving unlovely part of me.

Jesus died to take away our sins and redeem us for all eternity. If and when we accept his gift, he, and only he, can be the Savior of our lives. Forever. No one else can be that savior. If we filter seeing the world through the righteous cost of the cross, everything changes. The way we see someone else's selfishness will change. The way we see wrongness, and the sins of everyday life will change. And when our lens changes, our hearts change. When our hearts change, how and what we receive and give to others also changes. Only then will we be equipped to be a worthy disciple of the good news. Because we will know what the good news is really about and it has nothing to do with how someone treats us, or the circumstances of good and bad in our lives.

## A BLINDING DARKNESS

This chapter is specifically about anger, bitterness, and hate. How well acquainted are you with any of these? Have you ever experienced what I did that day? Have you forgiven and moved past it? What are you hanging onto that is unforgiven in your heart? What are the feelings you need to give over to the Lord?

Before that day all those years ago, I would have said I was not well acquainted with hate. I'm not by nature an angry person. Perhaps, I even felt a little above it, until I dug in and thought about hate on a different level and explored God's Word. 1st John 2:9 says, "Anyone who claims to be in the light but hates a brother or sister is still in the darkness," and (in verse 11), "They do not know where they are going, because the darkness has blinded them."

Most of us have tasted some form of bitterness in our lives. Bitterness is anger settled in for the ride, festering until it's uglier than anger. It is the darkness that blinds us. It blinded me from seeking God or wanting to make amends with Mike. Bitterness has to be one of the saddest states of one's heart, and we are to obliterate it as quickly as possible before it mushrooms out of control.

How do we rid ourselves of it when someone has wronged us?

How do we then handle the range of wrongs in our lives? A spouse cheats. A car cuts you off while driving. An adult child blocks you from their life. A friend hurts you. The neighborhood children encroach uninvited on your yard. These are examples which can lead to a range of emotions from annoyance to anger to hate to bitterness. There are hundreds of examples of us being wronged and they can all trigger the same selfish darkness in our hearts. The challenge we face, the one inside ourselves, has little to do with what others throw at us, good or bad.

The more we practice darkness, the more darkness creeps in. The more we carry bitterness, the more bitterness creeps in. How do we not let even little annoyances grate on us? I know people who are mad at everything and everyone. They walk through life entitled and owed. They are walking in a practice of darkness. They are not looking to love. They are looking only to be loved. They are not looking to give. They are looking only to receive. They are not looking to give grace, yet they expect it from others. It's the selfishness of the heart which seeks ourselves above all others.

## FORGIVENESS IS FOR YOU

As Christ-followers, we are to forgive. Jesus said to Peter, "Forgive seventy times seven" (Matt. 18:22, KJV...emphasis added). In this, Jesus doesn't mean you are to forgive 490 times and then stop. He is implying that we are to forgive over and over again. We aren't to put a limit on our forgiveness. Forgiveness doesn't mean allowing someone's sin to continue, especially one that is toxic or harmful to you. This isn't about the behaviors of another which we sometimes need to distance ourselves from. You may be called to distance from someone (because of harm), but even with distance, there's still a place for forgiveness. I have forgiven people (and hold no grudges) yet don't engage with them because it's not healthy or safe. This is not about acceptance of someone's unsafe darkness. This is about *our* hearts, the hearts we have to live with, which lean towards either darkness or light.

Luke 6:27–28 says, "Love your enemies, do good to those who

hate you, bless those who curse you, pray for those who mistreat you."

Living in the light means we see others in a different way. We notice who they are as a person first. The children playing uninvited in your yard are an opportunity to befriend. The driver who cuts you off (who is clearly in the wrong) is an opportunity for you to pray for their day (and not in anger). It's recognizing that the rude ticket counter person at the airport might be having a bad day and needs a little extra kindness. We recognize that even the ones who are toxic are valuable to God and have hope.

The spouse who cheats is also an opportunity. It may not seem like it, and clearly cheating is wrong and painful, but it's still an opportunity to look to God and his Word, because *everything* is an opportunity to look to God's Word. I'm not saying you're going to stay in your marriage, but I am saying that practiced bitterness has the potential to steal you away quicker than your spouse's cheating if you let it. Don't let it. Turn to God and his Word and ask the Spirit to guide you in rightness, in love, in forgiveness, and in light, whether you remain married or not. Our part of the equation of godliness is not determinant on another person's behaviors, as difficult and hurtful as those behaviors might be. Bitterness is darkness within us, and there's no place for it. Ever. For any reason. At any time.

Jesus felt my ugly bitterness that awful day at the airport. That day wasn't only about Mike's decision. It was as much about my part in it. My lack of honesty in speaking up to tell Mike I needed him (my pride got in the way). I felt weak and didn't want to admit it. I expected Mike to be my everything, and when he wasn't, it was my selfishness I lingered in. It was my turning away from God because it felt good in the moment to turn away. It was my indulgence of self rather than accepting the truths of Scripture. Jesus took on my sins that day. He knew the situation before I did. He knew it on the cross and he took my sin and nailed it along with all the others.

## SWEET VICTORY

Before you taste the sweet ugliness of hate and bitterness, think of the one who has already felt it, the one who died for it, and the one who will anguish over it. He's claimed and won the victory for us, and because he has, you can practice letting hate and bitterness go. God will work everything out according to his *good* purposes, the way he did for me all those twenty-five years ago. God showed me who I need to put my trust in. I now get it more right than wrong. I've practiced that day's lesson over and over again. I've needed reminded, of course, but thankfully, our God is a patient loving God.

You may not always *feel* like it, but you can choose to walk in this truth the next time anger tries to tell you you're right, and bitterness steps in to steal the show. The more you see Jesus, the less you'll feel wronged. The more you see Jesus, the more compassion you'll have for others, and the less you'll see of yourself. You won't care as much about the peripherals that used to trigger you. Anger, bitterness, hate, and all those "like" feelings will start to dissipate in your life and joy will find its way into your soul. There's such hope in this truth.

Psalm 30:11 says, "You have turned my mourning into dancing; you removed my sackcloth and clothed me with joy."

Make this your prayer. Fill in the blank for yourself, whatever your situation might be:

> *Jesus, Thank you for the cross. Turn my _______________ (anger, bitterness, sadness, hate, annoyance, impatience, intolerance) into dancing; remove the sackcloth of my sin and bad feelings and clothe me with joy. Amen.*

Lastly, if there are any men reading this, don't get on a plane without your wife or you're going to have to write the best apology note of your life.

# CHAPTER 7

## Study and Reflection

Bible verse: *1 Samuel 18:6-9* – Read.
Write out the 1st sentence in verse 18:8 in the space below:

_______________________________________________

_______________________________________________

_______________________________________________

_______________________________________________

Why did the song "displease Saul greatly"?

The story of Saul, from beginning to end, is a fascinating and sad one. Saul seems always to be a man for himself, but the story regarding David is his complete undoing. Saul can't get past the one person he needs to get past to give glory to God; himself.

Saul didn't start out the way he ended up. Earlier, in 1st Samuel 10:10 we find that "the Spirit of God came powerfully upon Saul," but in 1st Samuel 16:14, "the Spirit of the LORD had departed from Saul, and an evil spirit from the LORD tormented him."

Read and consider 1st Samuel 18:28-29.

These verses are among the saddest verses I could find in Saul's story (and there are many). "When Saul realized that the LORD was with David…he remained his enemy the rest of his days."

What did David do that was so terrible? David killed the Philistine, Goliath, and helped Saul's army have great success. David was best friends with Saul's son, Jonathan, and he married Saul's daughter Michal. The Lord was with David. There was every reason for Saul to align with David. To befriend him. To love him. To embrace him as a son. Saul had everything to gain, but his desire for power and fame got in the way, and in the end, it was his complete undoing.

It is a long story of betrayal, anger, bitterness, hatred, jealousy, and evil. Not because of what David did but because of Saul's heart. The slippery slope of wanting to elevate ourselves above others can so quickly turn our hearts to stone.

Are there times when we begrudge others who have more than we do? If so, what does that look like?

Read 1st Samuel 31:4-6. How did things end for Saul?

It was the bitterest of endings. Saul's sons (Jonathan, Abinadab, and Malki-Shua) died in battle, and Saul killed himself, all on the same day. Saul died in his bitterness. He died in his pride. He died in his evil. He died and his body was burned and that is the end of his sad story, except that it is forever preserved in God's Word.

*Lord, we read the story of Saul, and we think this can't possibly happen to us. We aren't as prideful, angry, hate-filled, or evil like Saul was. Yet, anger is anger. Pride is pride. Bitter is bitter. Sin is sin. We pray that you will keep our minds and our hearts from evil. Keep us pure in spirit. Help us to fix our hearts on Jesus, the perfector of our faith, so that we can and will build others up over and above ourselves and give the glory to God. Help us keep love in our hearts so bitterness doesn't steal it away. Yet your will be done. Amen.*

# 8

# Comfort: An Addiction to Avoid

*My name is Sheri Walker and I'm a comfort addict.*

I'm writing this chapter in winter, where a heated blanket covers my bed at night, and a space heater keeps me warm when I write in the morning. I eat a large salad for lunch every day with a protein of choice and the salad greens torn small. I have a favorite white towel, and once or twice a week, it gets washed and rehung on the same day. I use multiple kinds of toothpastes. I like a bright house with the lights on, which has all these years gone uncontested by a thrifty husband. I feel anxious when my phone's battery goes below fifty percent. I have more eggs than I know what to do with as I buy eight dozen each week from a local farmer and share with family and friends. I never run out of ripe avocados and at any given time, you'd find at least five in my refrigerator. I'm always stocked up with numerous flavors of Burt's Bees Lip Balm, and I've been on the hunt for chocolate, the grandkids' favorite.

I like. I want. I need. I have. I prefer. I never. I don't. I won't. My name is Sheri Walker and I'm a comfort addict. I like things a certain way and an empty nest, financial security, and the freedoms

I live with enable the comfort I'm accustomed to. In fact, you could call my life a comfort enabler. Mike and I have enough of everything we need, and we've grown into a life of comfort, and yes, it feels good (there's that *feel* word again). Comfort, sometimes more than anything else, threatens to keep me from my best godly self if I'm not careful.

What about you? Think through your days and weeks and consider all the things you're particular about. What is it that makes your life easier? Consider the things you'd hesitate or struggle to do without. Don't we all want the kind of comfort that eases our lives, removes pain, and well…makes us comfortable?

I don't think I'm different from others, although it's possible I'll write this chapter and expose myself as a comfort outlier. I'm willing to take the risk. I think I'm everybody, especially those who are more *mature*, or who may have finished raising children and are living with more financial security than when they were younger. The young have built-in discomforts. Parenting, by its very nature, brings discomfort. Kids, at any age, are hard. That's a fact of life. If you're raising children with special needs, you may have an above average level of discomfort. While Mike and I were raising our out-of-the-box children, we weren't comfortable, yet we were able to withstand our discomfort. Now that we're far removed from it, we can't imagine going back to it. Our current abundance of peace and calm has stolen our strength and resolve to withstand what we used to be able to withstand, although age has something to do with tolerance and strength, no doubt. Peace and calm and comfort have replaced discomfort, and there's no doubt, we relish in our comfort.

## MIRED IN COMFORT

I have to be aware of my propensity for all things *comfortable*. I have to push myself away from the call of it on my life. I don't want to be so mired in comfort that I fail to answer the higher calling of God. Mired means to be stuck, trapped, or ensnared. Can we really look at comfort (referring to easing our way of life as compared to easing a person's distress) as a kind of ensnaring? The answer is an absolute yes, we can.

Comfort is the perfect analogy to the Spotted Lanternfly I spoke of in chapter one. It's enticing, and we are deceived by its attractive lure, until we see the true nature of it. I fight against comfort consistently as I believe it steals me away from my faith, relationships, health and wellness, movement, serving, and kingdom work. I believe there is a direct dichotomy between the health of these aforementioned things and a life devoted, even subconsciously, to comfort. I'm not sure we can have both. I know I can't.

We are not to seek discomfort for the sake of chastising ourselves over comfort. I'm not going to give up my nice white towel and switch to a cheap threadbare towel. God loves us *and* yes, he brings us abundance and rest because he is a good God who loves his children. All good things, including white towels, are things to be grateful for. But, as we explore this propensity for our feelings to take front and center in our lives, we have to be cautioned that too much of a good thing may not be a good thing if it becomes the thing we most strive for. What we strive and long for reveals the heart. One of the definitions of religion is "a pursuit or interest to which someone ascribes supreme importance to." What we are driven towards is indicative of what's valuable to us, and I would urge, worthy of our consideration.

"The enemy comes in to steal, kill and destroy," (John 10:10). The enemy is Satan. Could his tactics come in the form of an easy chair, excessive entertainment, a nice healthy retirement, and all things *comfortable*? What about the rest of Jesus' statement in John 10:10, "I have come that you may have life, and have it to the full." Whoa, you say. This sounds as if Jesus is promoting the "good life," the kind of life I'm now trying to persuade you to guard against. But is Jesus' definition of abundance the same as our definition of abundance? Is it closer to Paul's definition in Ephesians 3:20 (ESV), "Now to him who is able to do far more abundantly than all that we ask or think, according to the power at work within us?" Are they the same kind of abundance? We can attempt to take John 10:10 on its own to mean what we want…until…until we read the rest of the Gospels, and *all* of the New Testament, and *all* of the Bible, and only then will we know that living life to "the full" for a believer is not about living your days out in comfort. Don't take my word for it…take the Word's word for it and see for yourself.

## THE GOSPEL'S DISCOMFORT

There are many verses or stories in the Bible which make us cringe in their apparent discomfort. What about the Beatitudes found in Matthew 5? They're a lesson in discomfort. Blessed are the poor in spirit. Blessed are those who mourn. Blessed are the meek, and those who are persecuted.

Jesus tells us, "The last will be first and the first will be last" (Matthew 20:16), and he talks about the idea of "pruning," or cutting off in us that which does not bear fruit. There's nothing comfortable about that idea.

Like the idea (in the *Feelings* chapter) of calling Jesus' teachings the "suffering gospel," perhaps we can also call God's Word the "discomfort gospel." The teachings of Scripture, from start to finish, are not where you will find all things comfortable. The stories in the Old Testament, and the teachings of Jesus, and Paul are almost a study in discomfort.

In my first book, I quoted Amy Carmichael, a missionary who saved hundreds of homeless children in India in the 1800's, when she said, "It is so fatally easy to forget that we are not here to enjoy life or live pleasantly."[3] What a strong statement. Is it really fatal to enjoy life, live pleasantly, and have abundance? I suppose it is if it takes us away from God and our role in his kingdom. I don't believe we can't enjoy life. I have found a joy I didn't know *because* of who I am in Christ. I live pleasantly. Yes, I face hardships, struggles, fear, worry, and all things human, but in between those things, I live pleasantly. I have a pleasant loving husband, and family, friends, and a home I enjoy. I don't consider these things sins or counter-biblical, and yet, I understand what Amy Carmichael is trying to say. She's trying to

---

[3] *A Chance to Die, The Life and Legacy of Amy Carmichael.* Elisabeth Elliot. 1987. Baker Publishing, Grand Rapids, MI

warn us not to let our enjoyment of life pull us so far that it becomes our religion. I know firsthand that comfort can be a "pursuit and interest," and we need to battle this pull like we battle anything that draws us away from being a worthy disciple of Jesus. Jesus told those around him to "sell everything you have, and then come, follow me" (Luke 18:22). Following Jesus is the antithesis of living a life in comfort.

## HOW DO WE HALT COMFORT'S DRAW?

As a believer, we need to know the Bible and seek who God is calling us to be and what he's calling us to do. We can eliminate ideas and terms from our vocabulary; terms like entitled, deserve, earned, and owed. We don't work hard to earn retirement or take it easy, at least not in Scripture. We work hard because it's what we're supposed to do throughout our lives. In God's Word, there's no end for this hard work, no culmination of "doing good." We've not earned the right to do nothing because we're older, or because we've worked hard all our lives, or because we've retired. Retirement isn't planned comfort. Instead, it should be redirection in other areas which have calling, meaning, value, and dare I say, hard work. We think of retirement as a time of rest. A time of stopping. Lounging. Comfort. Indulgence. I see it as a time of respite. Resting in spirit from one thing as we revitalize ourselves in something else. It can lead to income, or not, but either way, it's doing something of purpose and continuing on where the Spirit leads you next. Our great commission has no ending.

I have my own personal anecdote to comfort, and although I write about it in my first book (*Strong, From Here to Eternity*), it's worth briefly revisiting.

I have a rule of yes and I'm continually practicing it, especially when I feel the pull of comfort pressing in. It's been one of the biggest changes in me, as I work to not squander my abilities and time to serve others. Doing yourself what others could (or even should) be doing starts to become more instinctual. And the rule of yes keeps me active and moving.

Here are five basic questions I ask when deciding to do or not do something:

1. *Is it good for me?* It's important we don't place ourselves in bad or toxic circumstances which threaten to bring us down, threaten our safety, or impact us negatively.

2. *Is it good for others?* Once you've passed the first test, is it good for someone(s) else? This takes the focus off of us and seeks to think of others.

3. *Am I able to do it?* Am I physically, financially, morally, and spiritually able to do it? Ability is important when making decisions.

4. *Will it impact anyone negatively?* Our yesses shouldn't hurt or compromise another's well-being.

5. *Does it align with Scripture? Nothing* we do should contradict the inerrant truths of the Bible.

This rule of yes applies to anything. Changing diapers. Doing dishes. Taking a friend to the airport. Exercising. Helping a neighbor. Volunteering at church. Speaking.

It's an awareness that puts serving others front and center. Practiced enough times, you won't need to run your decisions through each question. Saying yes and serving will start to become second nature.

*If I can, I will.* Repeat after me. *If I can, I will.*

In a way, for me, it's delayed comfort. I have learned the practice and habit of delaying my comfort. I've practiced intermittent fasting for more than six years. It helped me lose excess weight and become healthy, because it taught me the principle of delayed gratification. I like to eat. I like to cook. I like food. But I needed to be healthier, and over time, I was able to successfully delay the comfort of eating (because of the health it brought to me). Saying yes to good things and serving others is more of the same. It's delayed comfort. Rest and comfort come later, after the work is done.

## RESPITE IS GOOD

Our best example of respite is Jesus. He pulled back to rest when he was tired. He filled up his reserves, but he didn't stop his mission. He continued on once his reserves were filled. Respite is a short rest from something difficult and draining. I'm not anti-rest. We all need a break. We need to fill our tanks. Mike and I filled ours with our few years of respite once life settled down. I retired from a much-too-busy career and started writing. God was pulling us back and filling up our reserves for the next chapter (no pun intended).

## LONGEVITY'S EXAMPLES

I recently met a vibrant happy Christian couple at a pool party, and in a group conversation they revealed their ages; ninety-one and ninety-two. I heard an audible gasp. No one would've guessed it. I couldn't help myself and I later cornered them and asked how they maintained such vibrant longevity. Their answer came in four main areas of their lives:

1. Moving/doing every day.
2. Daily inputting into someone else's life.
3. Always serving in some capacity.
4. Hanging around young people.

This particular couple didn't take to heart a culture's definition of retirement, and they still felt relevant in the kingdom. Perhaps this is the biggest secret of all. They were still relevant. The mere fact that they drove thirty minutes to a fourth of July party to honor a young man of thirty-five (whom they had previously mentored) and meet his new wife showed commitment, relevancy, care, and intention. In a society where we often dishonor the elderly and treat them as throwaways, I found a couple who don't see themselves as throwaways. They looked more vibrant, happy, and energetic than people half their age. I was encouraged by them. They are who I want to become. They made me look at myself and ask the question, "What if I have thirty-two more years to be relevant?"

What about you? Subtract your current age from ninety-two and ask yourself the same question I asked. "What if I have [...] more years to be vibrant and relevant?" What would that look like? How are you going to use your time? How can we better emulate a life of moving, doing, giving, and serving for Jesus and his kingdom? I can tell you this. It won't come at the footstool of an easy chair.

# CHAPTER 8

## Study and Reflection

Bible verse: *Romans 16* – Read.
Write out verse 16:12 in the space below:

_______________________________________________

_______________________________________________

_______________________________________________

_______________________________________________

In my first book, *Strong, From Here to Eternity*, I write about stewarding our body, mind, and spirit to the glory of God and the glory of his kingdom. The title of that chapter (4) is *Strong Like Mr. Rogers*, as I used Fred Rogers, an ordained minister, as an example of someone who gave his all in his calling to minister to children.

In *Strong*, I stated, "We are the sheep asked to follow the worthiest of Saviors who died for us, and in doing so, we can shape a life worthy of our calling"[4]

"A life worthy of our calling." What do you think this kind of life looks like?

Can we live life comfortably and still live worthily? It is not for me to answer for each of you. It is enough for me to answer for myself, and I have found that comfort does not align itself well with worthiness. It may be my greatest challenge. I so love my comfort.

Romans 16 might seem an obscure chapter, and yet, it's a standard we can rise to. In this chapter we see first, Phoebe, "a benefactor

---

[4] *Strong, From Here to Eternity*. Walker, Sheri. 2023. Walking Turtle Press. Page 49.

of many people." Benefactor, or in the KJV, servant. What we know about Phoebe is that she served.

What about Priscilla and Aquila. "They risked their lives for me [Paul]."

What about Mary, Tryphena, Tryphosa, and Persis? They were "women who worked hard in the Lord."

Serving. Risking. Working. These are antitheses to comfort. Do we struggle to choose them over being comfortable? Why?

What are the areas of comfort that keep you from serving, risking, and working for the Lord?

Comfort isn't wrong, per say, but don't let it rule you. Don't let it be the deterrent to practicing giving yourself to the glory and love of God and others. Don't let it be the thing that keeps you from doing kingdom work.

Remember, our challenge is to see ourselves as an unfinished, grace-beholden treasure of God, befit to be and do and give until we can no longer be and do and give.

> *Lord, thank you for the ability to serve in the ways you lead us to serve. Help us overcome those things which threaten to impede our efforts, comfort being one of them. Don't let comfort rule our desires to such a point that we miss out on the good things you have for us. Help us to develop a practice of good yesses as we notice the opportunities you put in our path. Yet your will be done. Amen.*

# 9

# Perfectionism: A New 80/20 Rule

*Wading in the waters of perfectionism means we don't make a splash in the world.*

One of the roles in my past career was to occasionally craft our company's written materials. I once wrote an event speech for the owner, and she said I knew her better than she knew herself. I was proud of my speech-writing abilities, but mostly I assisted with emails when asked. I carefully wrote out diplomatic responses for others to send to clients, vendors, or anyone needing a more sensitive answer. In the highly volatile real estate business, how you say something is often more important than what you say. I was the voice of reason when emotions ran high. I was able to successfully put out fires with words on a page. Behind the scenes, however, my co-workers had no idea of the inordinate amount of time each *simple* email took me to write. Hours and hours. I'm almost embarrassed to admit, one normal email, needing the *touch* could easily take me a couple of hours, and even then, I'd leave it only to come back and tweak it later. I poured myself over every word and every phrase, making sure it was perfect, always reluctant to press send. Nothing I wrote was ever good enough. Letting go has been a problem for me. I've mostly managed the problem, but it still crops up.

If you think crafting an email is time-consuming, try crafting a book. Try taking a thousand ideas and sentences and words and figuring out how to craft them perfectly. How to say something just right, without mistakes, trying to let words go when they might not stick the landing. I have often lived in a place of never good enough. I used to be paralyzed by it. Pushing send meant there would be no more opportunities to make it better. I hated the inability to make something better. I hated to push send. I hated imperfect. Sometimes I still hate it. I've always been my own worst critic.

What about you? What prevents you from putting your work out into the world? It looks like fear, but is it based in something else? I'd call it a simple case of good old-fashioned pride. When you get right down to it, we find ourselves stuck in the pride of perfectionism because we don't want others to think badly of us. I was encouraged to feed my perfectionism because of the applause of others. The co-workers I wrote for not only thanked me, but built my efforts up with compliments, which I can see in hindsight had consequences. Compliments made me more prideful, which made me more careful, which took more time and effort, and I would argue, made others less capable or willing to do the work themselves.

## PERFECTIONISM WILL COST YOU

There is a cost for perfectionism. Perfectionism is a cycle that needs to be broken because it robs us of time, courage, and impact. We need courage to put ourselves out there, and we need to put ourselves out there to impact those around us. I'm convinced there's a whole bunch of closet dreamers. Closet writers, artists, speakers, teachers, and creatives who have something wonderful to offer. I'm convinced of this because I used to be one of them. The world needs those closet dreamers to leave the closet. God disciples through his people and each discipleship is unique because our gifts are unique. We can't disciple if we're stuck in our perfect thoughts of what it has to look like, paralyzed by perfection, or paralyzed by watching someone else do it (someone else, by the way, who pushed send and started). How do we change and get beyond ourselves?

One day it all changed for me with a conversation I had with a friend about her 80/20 rule. Not the one you're thinking of where twenty percent of the people make eighty percent of the income. Or twenty percent of the workers produce eighty percent of the work. Wilfredo Pareto, in 1897, noticed twenty percent of the pea pods in his garden produced eighty percent of the peas. (I thought that interesting and funny enough to inform you of). His theory was evaluated and expanded over the years by numerous others until the 80/20 rule became a thing. I'm not talking about *that* 80/20 rule. There's another rule I want you to consider, one which has greatly relieved my pressures of perfectionism, at least to the degree that allows me to push send.

My friend accurately sensed how crippling perfectionism was for me, understanding full well that perfection is unattainable and prevents moving forward and trying new things, and because she herself had to overcome it. I understood this to a degree but couldn't define why I got so stuck and consumed by perfectionism. She told me to let my work go when it's eighty percent and not worry about the other twenty percent. She said eighty percent was good enough. Good enough? That sounded like blasphemy to me. How dare anyone think good enough is good enough. It was *not* an idea I was initially comfortable with. Not be a hundred percenter? Put something out there that isn't my best? But the more we talked, the more it made sense, and in a way, gave me hope.

I started to see that I was practicing being paralyzed by fear. Fear of not getting it right. Fear of not living up to others' expectations. Fear of failure. Fear of looking stupid. Most things we put out into the world are never as critically analyzed the way we think they will be. People aren't sitting around just waiting for you to screw up. Most people don't care about your stuff because they have their own stuff to care about.

My friend's theory started to make sense to me, and it changed me. It was clear she knew me better than I knew myself. I started to see my world differently. Being eighty percent gave me a different kind of permission. Eventually, I spent less time doing the same tasks, worried less about what others thought, and trusted in *good enough* outcomes.

## SIMPLE CONCEPT WITH A BIG IMPACT

I'm amazed at how some of the simplest concepts are the impetus to changing a whole mindset. The 80/20 rule is that kind of concept and it worked to change me for good. It's now an overriding theme for me to keep moving. Let it go. Get it done. Stop being afraid. Stop living in my head. Stop striving for a perfection which has no hope of being realized. Be ok with making mistakes. I've had to learn to be vulnerable enough to make mistakes. So, it is with this book and my first book. I had to let them both go.

Writing books is one thing, but speaking is a whole different game, and speaking might have paralyzed the old me. I pray over my nerves and ask God to take my pride of perfectionism away, and take myself out of my messages, and instead, focus on the women who are there seeking encouragement and wisdom. I see myself as a conduit, hoping to inspire others to be drawn to Jesus and the Word. Inspiring others has become my driver and because it is, little can deter me. Not being over sixty years old. Not my inadequacies. Not my inexperience. Not my mistakes. Not my pride of needing to be perfect or strong enough. I've learned it's not my strength I'm walking in. It's the victory of Jesus which lasts far beyond me, my messages, and my weaknesses.

This principle doesn't suggest taking a less-than-your-best approach. Certainly, I work hard to make sure my books are readable, flow well, and say what I want them to say without grammatical, thematic, or theological mistakes. I do the necessary hard work to prepare talks for speaking events. I still shoot for excellence. Excellence is different from perfect. Perfect is unachievable. Excellence is achievable. There might be a gray line between the two but with practice, I've discovered the difference. The difference is doing the hard work, and then not holding on too tightly to it.

## THERE'S ONLY ONE PERFECT

The definition of biblical grace is undeserved favor. We don't have to be perfect in order for God to accept us. God is perfect. God knew we couldn't be perfect so he sent his son, Jesus, in human form to come to this earth and take on what we can't do on our own. We are unable to be sinless, yet, as Jesus took on our inability to be sinless, he says he'll be sinless for us. He has redeemed our sinful nature so we can be perfected in him.

Jesus says in Scripture to "be perfect as your heavenly father is perfect" (Matt. 5:48). The Greek word for perfect here is *telios*, meaning brought to its end, completed. That's what Jesus did for us, and yes, we are to strive for a holy perfection, even though we will come up short. We are only made perfect through the death and resurrection of Jesus. He is our perfection.

## GO MAKE A SPLASH

Are you living in fear of needing to get it one hundred percent right? Is your fear stopping you from fulfilling a dream? Is it stopping you from starting something new and exciting? Are you being held back by the same false thinking I used to have? And sadly, if you are, do you think others are missing out on something you can offer to them?

Wading in the waters of perfection means we don't make a splash in this world. If God is leading us to splash, then we need to splash and not worry about the ripples. He'll take care of the ripples. Moses argued a few times with God about not being good enough to bring the Israelites out of Egypt (Ex. 3–4). Moses said, "Who am I that I should go to Pharaoh and bring the Israelites out of Egypt? (3:11), and again (4:10–13), "Lord, I have never been eloquent, neither in the past nor since you have spoken to your servant. I am slow of speech and tongue," and, "Please send someone else." How did God respond? The Bible says, "The LORD's anger burned against Moses" (4:14). God was angry that Moses doubted the plan. Did Moses act in fear or pride? Could it have been both? He didn't feel good enough, and in that feeling, he failed to trust God.

The pride of perfectionism is a practice in trusting ourselves over trusting God. The practice of letting go is about trusting "God to work for the good of those who love him, who have been called according to his purpose" (Rom. 8:28). The 80/20 rule released my fears and helped me move forward with trusting God. I had to learn to trust that God could bring anything to fruition despite my inadequacies.

So it is, if you are reading this, you are getting my eighty percent best. Because if you weren't, you'd be getting nothing. In fact, Susan, my friend and writing partner, told me to practice what I preach when I read her this chapter (she said it nicer). It's a constant battle to put out eighty percent but I'm doing it anyway. My work will never be quite good enough, and that's ok. It's really ok.

## YOU HAVE PERMISSION

This chapter is about giving you permission to live your own eighty percent life, and not be paralyzed by the fear of not getting it perfectly right. It will *feel* uncomfortable and wrong and messy. I sometimes still push send with my eyes closed, telling myself it's good enough and to "let it go." But I know my imperfect eighty percent might make a difference in someone's life. What about you? What are you waiting for? Get out of your own way and let your eighty percent go out into the world. Don't let your perceptions of what others think stop you, or to put it differently, stop hiding your bright light under the proverbial bushel of perfectionism. Be who God is calling you to be. Go make a splash. You might be surprised by the ripples that follow.

# CHAPTER 9

## Study and Reflection

Bible verse: *2 Timothy 3:17* – Read.
Write out in the space below:

_______________________________________________

_______________________________________________

_______________________________________________

_______________________________________________

Who is it that equips us for every good work?

Perfectionism is a close cousin, if not a direct offspring of pride and shame, and is to be obliterated in the kingdom. It's perhaps more subtle than pride and shame, but just as effective at gaining a hold on our hearts.

In the book, *The War of Art*, author Steven Pressfield writes about resistance. He says, "Resistance cannot be seen, touched, heard, or smelled. But it can be felt. We experience it as an energy field radiating from a work-in-potential. It's a repelling force. It's negative. Its aim is to shove us away, distract us, prevent us from doing our work."[5]

Is there anything in your life where this idea of perfectionism is preventing you from moving forward with something God is calling you to do?

Can you see how perfectionism goes hand-in-hand with pride and shame?

---

[5] *The War of Art*. Steven Pressfield. 2002. Black Irish Entertainment. P. 7.

Write out 1ˢᵗ Peter 4:10.

_______________________________________________

_______________________________________________

_______________________________________________

_______________________________________________

What does a faithful steward do?

This chapter on perfectionism is written for me and for anyone who lingers too long in the presence of feeling like you're never good enough…long enough to be stuck there…long enough so that your gifts are being squelched…long enough so that no one is gaining what you have to offer.

Obviously, this chapter is not about an exact 80%. That's not something which can be defined. It's about being brave enough to let go and know Jesus is enough, so you don't have to be. He has already made you enough.

> _Lord, thank you for the gifts you have graciously given to each of us. Help us to not be so steeped in perfectionism that we empower resistance to shut down the splashes we can make in this world. You are the perfecter of our faith and every good gift we have. We offer up those good gifts as a sacrifice to you and a witness for others. Yet your will be done. Amen._

# THE CHALLENGE OF CIRCUMSTANCE

*"In him we were also chosen, having been predestined according to the plan of him who works out everything in conformity with the purpose of his will, in order that we, who were the first to put our hope in Christ, might be for the praise of his glory."*
Ephesians 1:11–12

# 10

# Under His Care

*I don't believe in coincidence, nor is it promoted anywhere in the Bible.*

Corrie Ten Boom, a Dutch watchmaker, was arrested on Feb 28, 1944, along with her father Casper, her sister Betsie, and thirty-five others for not disclosing the whereabouts of six Jews hidden in a secret room attached to Corrie's bedroom. Over the prior two-year period, the Ten Booms helped save over 800 Jews and/or Nazi-resisters. Casper and Betsie died in the concentration camps, but Corrie was released due to a clerical error. The week after her release, the Nazi's executed all women her age. Corrie went on to write the well-known book, *The Hiding Place*, as well as eight other books, and spoke in more than sixty countries. She called her release from the concentration camp "a human error and a miracle of God."[6] What do you think? Was it providential that Corrie was released?

## PROVIDENCE, HAPPENSTANCE, AND CHOICE

*Providence* is that which is by divine foresight or intervention. *Happenstance* is that which happens by chance, accident, or coinci-

---

[6] Ten Boom, Corrie. 2008. I Stand at the Door and Knock. Grand Rapids, Michigan: Zondervan. P. 23.

dence. *Choice* is what we decide when faced with two or more possibilities. How do we view each of these within our faith?

There are circumstances (or situations) we can't change and those we can. I can't change my birthday, who my parents are, or being 5 ft. 2 inches short. I couldn't change my mother's death, my brain tumor, or the four miscarriages I suffered. We can't change whether we are born into wealth or poverty, gifted with creativity or athleticism, or the size of our feet. And yet there are many circumstances we have control over. In most cultures, we decide who to marry. We decide on a career path. We decide what outfit to wear each day. We decide when to go to bed and when to rise. These kinds of choices are (usually) within our control.

Most of my life, I was in the camp which viewed circumstances as either self-imposed *choices* (we bring upon ourselves) or *happenstance* (happens by chance, accident, or coincidence). I didn't understand that *all* circumstances are within the providence of God. *All* circumstances. I don't believe in coincidence, nor is it promoted anywhere in the Bible. Happenstance, by biblical definition, is not a thing.

What does God's Word say about circumstances? So much it would have your head spinning. Too much for me to tackle in one short chapter, so I'm going to leave you with a few ideas. Remember, I'm the explorer giving thought to the ideology of such things so we can think and search the depth and riches of God's Word for ourselves.

Why should we explore these concepts? Why spend time considering our circumstances? Earlier, I made the statement that emotions, circumstances, and culture can't be placed neatly in their own category, but all intermingle together. Our circumstances have the capability to cause our emotions to ride the wind, up and down. You get angry and yell at your three-year-old for acting like a three-year-old. Someone cuts in front of you at the grocery store and you become irritated. You hang onto bitterness because of someone else's actions towards you. Your emotions flow according to the circumstances of the day and there's nothing to steady you. You're a slave to both.

My hope is that once you consider and filter your circumstances through God's truths, you'll be encouraged to see that *everything* is not only within the providence of God, but is being worked out continually in your favor, for your good. You may define good differently than God defines good, but nonetheless, for your good. Once you see life the way God does, you will also see how "The LORD will keep you from all harm – he will watch over your life; the LORD will watch over your coming and going both now and forevermore" (Psalm 121:7–8). When you know God, you'll see he can be trusted, and when you claim trust in the Lord, you'll be like Paul, who faced more ups and downs than anyone could, and yet was a steady follower and disciple, continually relinquishing his own life for the glory of God.

When you choose to live with God's purpose and destiny in mind, you'll find you no longer live dependent on good circumstances to provide your happiness.

## FORWARD WHYS

We think it's *happenstance* when a bolt of lightning hits a tree and splits it open. When lightning hits, we respond. We cower in fear or become angry. We might do nothing, which by the way, is a response. We fix the problem, like chopping down the tree and using the wood for kindling. There's a range of responses for each circumstance we face.

Do we need to know why the lightning hit the tree? Can we accept the fact that it did, and then get to work cleaning it up? Can we not linger so long in the past, but fix the present and seek out a better future? Can we refocus our lens to see that the why of our circumstances is less valuable than the responses we give to them?

I didn't ask why it poured on our wedding day. I didn't ask why I had four miscarriages, or why I had a brain tumor, or why the flight got canceled, or just yesterday, why I was stuck for an extra half hour in a traffic jam. There are a million important and unimportant whys I have no control over and have not concerned myself over. I'm a forward seeker, and as such, I'm always well…seeking forward and trying to make the best of a situation. I've admittedly thought of why as a bit of a dirty word. A weak position. A worthless exercise. An unhealthy focus. I saw why as an emotional trap designed to keep one stuck in the past rather than help one move forward with a solution.

Until now. More recently, I've filtered life through why, but it's not a backwards why which asks, "Why did this happen to me?" but instead a forward why. "Why does God have me in this situation and what does he want me to do about it?" *Why me* is me-centric, and *why God* is God-centric.

It's a powerful perspective change to see life through the lens of a loving and purposeful God. He loves me, knows every single thing about me (and my circumstances), and is there to protect and guide me rightly. With this thought, I've changed the way I view the happenings in my day. If God loves me and wants good things for me, I get to search for the good in the not-so-pleasant, and even awful, circumstances.

The practice of seeking God's goodness has increased my trust and reliance on God, and disappointments have all but disappeared from my *feelings*, or at a minimum, been greatly diminished. Disappointment is unmet expectations of what we want and think we can control. What if we viewed our unmet expectations as circumstances within the sovereignty of a knowing and loving God? One who has a better, higher purpose for the circumstance we find ourselves in? One who knows, sees, and "works all things out for the good of those who love him?" (Rom. 8:28). One who already knows our destiny?

## A PURPOSEFUL BOLT

What does it look like to ask why forward? Could the lightning bolt have hit the tree because God protected the house? Instead of feeling frustrated in a traffic jam, could it be that travel is delayed for a good reason? Could I have gotten a brain tumor to slow me down, refocus my priorities, become serious about God, *and* see health and wellness as a worthy life commitment? Could the tumor have strengthened the days I have left, even as it weakened the days I suffered through it? Have the difficulties with our youngest daughters been an impetus to draw me closer to God and care for others in similar circumstances? Can a life-altering devastating pandemic refocus millions of lives, change society, and bring many to Jesus? Well? Could it?

Could our troubles have a meaning beyond what we can see or know in our tiny little minds? If so, could they change the way we think and act? Could they change the essence of who we are in Christ?

In the life of the believer, every little and big thing is a situation within the providence and goodness of God. Nothing is too small or inconsequential for him. No traffic jam. No poor night's sleep. No trip to the grocery store. No lightning bolt. God knows every single part of our lives, and it's in every single part he's seeking surrender, not to our circumstances, but to him. To the higher calling of seeing Christ *within* every aspect of our lives.

What about horrible things? Death. Suicide. Illness. Financial crisis. Divorce. Loss of a child. Surely, these can't be under the providence of a loving Father. I don't know the mysteries of God and how he "works everything out for good," but if the Bible is inerrant (it is), and God is sovereign, then he knows us, loves us, and works it *all* out for eternity.

God knows everything about us…every thought…every circumstance…everything. "Even the very hairs of your head are all numbered" (Matt. 10:30). He knows what you're thinking as he tells you to "take captive every thought to make it obedient to Christ" (2 Cor. 10:5). He knows and is there to guide and love and draw us to himself and the One he sent to save us. That's our destiny over every good, bad, and horrific circumstance we face.

## GOD IS OUR STRONG TOWER

The message of Psalm 139:1–3 is that God knows us. "You have searched me, LORD, and you know me. You know when I sit and when I rise; you perceive my thoughts from afar. You discern my going out and my lying down; you are familiar with all my ways."

Don't stop there. Continue on to verses 4–5, "Before a word is on my tongue you, LORD, know it completely. You hem me in behind and before, and you lay your hand upon me."

Finally, in verses 23–24, "Search me, God, and know my heart;

test me and know my anxious thoughts. See if there is any offensive way in me and lead me in the way everlasting."

David wrote this Psalm (and many others) under great oppression, running for his life, and hiding from his father-in-law, King Saul, who wanted to murder him and seize his growing power. David's circumstances were crushing, and yet he continued to seek God.

This is an example of asking why forward. The Psalms David wrote are a beautiful study in safety, sanctuary, security, protection, refuge, salvation, and love. "You [God] are my refuge, a strong tower against the foe" (Psalm 61:3). David was always looking to God in the midst of his strife.  Perhaps this is one of the reasons God calls David, "a man after my own heart" (1 Sam. 13:14).

2nd Corinthians 4:17 says, "For our light and momentary troubles are achieving for us an eternal glory that far outweighs them all." What are "light and momentary troubles?" A traffic jam? A miscarriage? A pandemic? A sleepless night? Cancer? Could it be all of these and more?

What if we take every part of the good and bad of our lives and filter them through God's providence and care? What if, instead of focusing on *our* needs, wants, and desires, we focused instead on *God's*? Could this way of thinking take the focus (and burden) off us?

If we answer yes to these questions, we'll find peace on the other side – and a more accepting attitude when something doesn't go according to plan. Disappointment and anxiety are a lack of trust in what God has for us.

## A DIFFERENT LENS

A friend, stressed over a trivial matter, came to me for advice. I tried to refocus her to what really mattered, and it *wasn't* the trivial thing she was irritated with. As I reminded her of what was most important in life, I saw her tension visibly leave her. She said, "I'm impressed with the way you seem to take life in stride and not let things bother you. I wish I could be more like that."

The thing is, she *can* be more like that. We all can. I'm not the same person I used to be. I see most interruptions in life as trivial and not worth worrying about. Facing crisis changed my lens. I don't care much about fairness anymore, and I've learned to see something favorable in most situations, eliminating many of the cares, worries, disappointments, and annoyances that used to grate on me. Illness revealed how short life is, the unimportance of unimportant things, the gift of joy, and the presence of God in ordinary everyday life.

I also don't see success the same way I used to. God has taught me to focus on him and the work at hand. I know God has preordained my outcomes, and I'm content to leave it in his hands. Many would think me foolhardy for some of my restrained choices, but the Spirit impresses upon me the work to be done, and my job is to put my head down and comply. I read, pray, research, think, write, and speak. It doesn't mean I never get distracted, but I'm cognizant of staying the course because I know if I get off the track of obedience, I'm going to miss the goodness God has for me.

## THE REFINING PROCESS

There was a man who had no family, and his work became his family. He worked hard, yet was never satisfied, his thirst never quenched as he worked harder and harder. At some point in his life journey, he asked himself, "Why am I working so hard? Why am I depriving myself of better things? It's all so meaningless. My wealth and my business mean nothing without enjoyment…without love." This is the lesson of Ecclesiastes 4:8, and it was a lesson I learned for myself. It was the fast-tracking-sanctified-holy-making-refining process in my life. I'm thankful for a loving Father whose persistence showed me that what I thought was important wasn't important. He takes the broken pieces of our lives and refines them through life circumstances.

God also says in Ecclesiastes 3:11, "God has made everything beautiful in its time. He has set eternity in the human heart; yet no one can fathom what God has done from beginning to end."

We can't fathom how God will bring everything in our lives together. We can't really understand how he will work it out for our good. We can, however, hold on to God's truths. We can think on them and hold them close to our hearts, reminding ourselves daily that we are under his care. We'll have to hold on tightly though because day by day we're being tested, and this is part of God's plan as well.

# CHAPTER 10

Bible verse: *2 Samuel 18:33* – Read.
Write out the first 2 sentences in the space below:

___________________________________________________

___________________________________________________

___________________________________________________

___________________________________________________

Earlier in this chapter, I wrote that "David's circumstances were crushing, and yet he continued to seek God." As I write about our circumstances under the care of a loving God, I don't want us to think there's no room for sorrow and sadness. Here, in our verse in 2nd Samuel, we see a very shaken David. He cried over his son, Absalom, who had just been killed. David and Absalom had a strained relationship (to put it mildly), but a son is a son, and David loved Absalom.

Upon hearing about Absalom's death, we read (2 Sam. 18:33–19:4) that David mourned, wept, grieved, covered his face, and cried aloud.

Ecclesiastes (3:4) tells us there is a season for everything, including "a time to weep and a time to mourn."

I don't want us to think that holding onto the truths of a sovereign God and being under his providential care doesn't mean we can't grieve or be sad. We're not robots. We're called to times of immense suffering, and that suffering calls for times of grief.

How much time? Certainly, that varies from person to person and situation to situation. There are no set rules for grieving. When I had each of my four miscarriages, I discovered I grieved differently from some others who went through the same circumstances. I cried my eyes out for a couple of days, and then moved on rather quickly. My nature is and has always been to accept the things I can't control and move forward.

How we grieve is not as important as *that* we grieve, and grieving is a gift. Jesus said, "Blessed are those who mourn" (Matt. 5:4). Why are they blessed? Because "they will be comforted" (5:4).

Psalm 34:18 tells us, "The LORD is close to the brokenhearted and saves those who are crushed in spirit." It was David who wrote this Psalm. David knew how to be under God's care *and* experience times of being crushed and brokenhearted.

We are called to trust a providential God, and it's warranted to feel the intensity of our losses and our suffering and pain with all the feelings God has entrusted to us.

> *Lord, thank you for showing us that it's ok to grieve and still trust in your care of us at the same time. Thank you for being close to the brokenhearted. We trust that we can leave our lives in your capable hands…under your providential care through everything we have to face in life. Yet your will be done. Amen.*

# 11

## How to Survive the Sifting

*It was the LORD's will to crush him and cause him to suffer.*

I write and speak often of my brain tumor because it changed my life, but the ongoing crises which brought me lower than anything else was raising daughters with trauma, anger, and aggression. Trying to fix their brokenness has been the journey of twenty-three years and a thousand miles of pain and heartbreak, both theirs and ours.

I understand what PTSD feels like. I've changed my phone's ring tone because a certain tone causes my heart to race. I don't look at photo memories when they pop up on my phone in case there's one that triggers a painful memory. I've gotten rid of items that remind me of bad times. It's been more than six years since Mike and I have slept with a locked bedroom door at night, and I sometimes still look at the open door and breathe a grateful sigh of relief over our current peace and calm, amazed at how long we lived without.

I used to belong to a RAD (Reactive Attachment Disorder) Facebook group and had to leave it. I couldn't listen to hopeless stories from hopeless parents filled with endless pain, accompanied too often with hateful rhetoric. Over the years, Mike and I have met with many parents who experienced similar struggles as ours. One time, I met and sat with a mom for five hours as she poured her heart out to me regarding her hostile out-of-control teenager. Five hours. At which point, I'm ashamed to say I lied to her and told her I had to be somewhere. I didn't know how to be honest without being hurtful. She left and I laid down, emotionally worn out from not only taking on her pain but triggering my own. It wasn't the first time I ministered to someone else while it emotionally drained me. Sometimes this is the cost of listening. I'm glad to be a listener, but it's the reason I have not yet entered the mission field to help parents like us. Yet. If the Lord wants me in that field, he'll remove the triggers. I'll know if and when that day comes, but for now, I'm not there. It's still all too close.

## SLOBBERKNOCKERED

I know I'm not alone when I speak to the difficulties and unexpected curve balls that life throws at you. Curve balls that have you slobberknockered, taking a proverbial bat to the head. Like Job. Yes, I'm back to Job. He's the perfect example of being slobberknockered. Remember…he lost everything. His ten children, his position, wealth, respect, and eventually his health. His wife became bitter (she lost everything too), and his friends were critical of him. Job wanted to die. There was nothing left for him. "Sighing has become my daily food; my groans pour out like water. What I feared has come upon me; what I dreaded has happened to me. I have no peace, no quietness; I have no rest, but only turmoil" (Job 3:24–25).

I have not suffered to the extent Job did, but I relate to him when he says. "I have no peace, no quietness; only turmoil." Have you ever felt this way? Have you ever asked, isn't enough, enough?

God answers Job's distress in five chapters (Job 38:42), "Who is this that obscures my plans with words without knowledge?" (38:2), and "Who has a claim against me that I must pay? Everything under heaven belongs to me" (41:11). Job answers God, "I know that you can do all things; no purpose of yours can be thwarted. Surely, I spoke of things I did not understand, things too wonderful for me to know" (42:2–3).

"Wonderful" or "wonder" in the original Greek/Hebrew language is the word *pala* which means "beyond one's power, difficult to understand, extraordinary, or marvelous."[7] "There are other places in the Bible which talk about the kind of "wonderful" Job is referring to. In Psalm 139:6, David says, "Such knowledge is too wonderful for me, too lofty for me to attain." Deuteronomy 29:29 calls it "secret" things that only God knows, secret things best left for God alone. God is telling Job he [God] is in charge, and Job is in essence saying back to God, "You're right God. It's all too much for me to know. No purpose of yours can be prevented." Job not only admits he doesn't understand, but admits his life is under God's authority, not his own.

Raising children with trauma, and the brain tumor were *pala* moments for me. At sixty-one years old, one thing I can count on is experiencing things "too wonderful for me to know." Hardships. Loss. Suffering. Pain.

In the previous chapter, we turned *why me* around to seek God's purposes in our circumstances. But there's another why question I ask myself when life seems unfair or overwhelming, and it's one that keeps me grounded. Why *not* me?

## WHY NOT US?

Why should you and I be any different from Job? Why should we be any different from Corrie Ten Boom? Why should we be any different from Elisabeth Elliot? Why should you and I be any different from them and the many other biblical and contemporary saints? Could our hardships (as desperate as we are to be rid of them) be the impetus to a stronger faith and a stronger witness? Psalm 90:12 (NLT) says, "Teach us to realize the brevity of life, so that we may grow in wisdom." This was the prayer God gave to Moses to impart to the people of Israel shortly before he died. This verse could be my mission statement. It's one of the most valuable lessons I've learned as I've not wanted to squander life away. Reminding myself that life is short helps me to live it to its fullest.

---

[7] https://www.bibletools.org/index.cfm/fuseaction/Lexicon.show/ID/H6381/pala.htm

## AN ORDAINED SUFFERING

We have explored the concept of everything being under the care of God, but I want to go further. I want us to consider a question I've deeply pondered. Does God allow and ordain (order, appoint, control) suffering in order to seize and accelerate our faith? Did God ordain and foresee how difficult my journey would be with my girls? Did he appoint a paralyzing brain tumor? Did God ordain these things (and others) to happen? Does a good God allow us to experience pain and suffering as a way to draw us closer to him? Is this what pruning looks like? Do we believe God when he tells Job, "Everything under heaven belongs to me." And remember, God says Job's circumstances are "my plans."

I hope God cares about the state of my heart even to the extent of allowing and ordaining something painful in my life. The truth is, God cares more about the state of our hearts than the happiness and comfort of our days. 1st Peter 5:10 (ESV) says, "After you have suffered a little while, the God of all grace, who has called you to his eternal glory in Christ, will himself restore, confirm, strengthen, and establish you."

Suffering is part of the plan. It's the story of Job. It's the thorn in Paul's side. It's what Joseph had to go through. It's the waiting of Abraham and Sarah for their promised baby. It's the trials of Moses and Jonah and Ruth and the disciples. It's the story of Corrie and Elisabeth and Amy. It's my journey of parenting, my brain tumor, and everything I've been through.

It's the plight of Jesus who was appointed to die for all who would come to believe and be saved. If the pain and suffering and death of Jesus was appointed by a loving Father, then Jesus is our great example. The cross didn't just happen to Jesus. He was born to it. He was ordained for it. That's the reason he came. In Isaiah 53:5 (KJV), it says, "Christ was bruised for us," and in verse 10, "It pleased the LORD to bruise him." Or in the NIV, "It was the LORD's will to crush him and cause him to suffer." Christ was bruised in order for us to be saved, and so also, we are bruised in order to be made holy. James 1:2 not only tells us to "count it all joy," but is followed by telling us that testing produces steadfastness (v.3), and steadfastness is where we will be made "perfect and complete" (v.4).

I stand corrected from my first book (I'm far from perfect), when I said, "God didn't give me the brain tumor, but he surely protected me when I got it." I can no longer rely on this statement. I can't know what God did or didn't give me, and even if he didn't give it to me, it surely passed through his sovereign hands. Remember happenstance? There's no such thing in Scripture.

## SIFTED AS WHEAT

In Luke 22:31, Jesus says to Peter, "Satan has asked to sift all of you as wheat." In the Greek, the word "asked" is harsher, translated as "demanded." Satan is demanding to shake up Peter and the other disciples' faith. How does Jesus respond? He tells Peter, "I have prayed for you, Peter, that your faith may not fail." Notice what Jesus doesn't say. He doesn't say, "I won't give permission for you to be sifted." No, Jesus says, "I'll pray that you survive the sifting."

Wheat is sifted so the husk or outer shell, called the chaff, can be removed to get to the wheat berries which are then refined to flour. Sifting is not a gentle process nor a quick one (especially if you are doing it by hand). You must break the hard outer shell in order to get to the good useful nutritional part. *In order to...* Don't miss this point. It's the perfect metaphor for us as we are broken down to become refined. Broken down in order to get to the good useful part of us.

"I'll pray that you survive the sifting." As all-knowing and all-powerful in every way, God has the power to prevent the sifting. He could have protected the disciples from going through everything they went through. But would protection from everything difficult and painful have molded, refined, strengthened, and perfected them in Christ?

Later in the New Testament, Paul tells us he was "given his thorn, the messenger of Satan, to harass him so he wouldn't become conceited" (2 Cor. 12:7 – emphasis added). Who allowed Paul's thorn?

God. Why? To keep him humble. We can assume pride was a place of weakness for Paul, and because it was, he needed to be kept from it.

"God's power is made perfect in weakness" (2 Cor. 12:9). God is sovereign. Everything passes through him. He has a predetermined plan, and my troubles are part of the plan. God has ordained me to be sifted as wheat. I find it an honor to follow in the footsteps of his disciples because I am one of them, and like the disciples, I have an enemy in Satan and his demons.

The devil is out to get me and you. You might find this language uncomfortable, and I understand. It *is* uncomfortable. Perhaps, like me, you were raised to sidestep Satan. Pretend he doesn't exist. Focus on the love of God and the forgiveness of sins. But to do *only* that would be to ignore the wisdom and warnings of Scripture. C.S. Lewis said, "There are two equal and opposite errors into which our race can fall about the devils. One is to disbelieve in their existence. The other is to believe, and to feel an excessive and unhealthy interest in them."[8] Paul tells us to "not give the devil an opportunity" (Eph. 4:27 NASB). If we are to not give him an opportunity, we must know how he works. A foundational knowledge in the Word helps us recognize how and why we're being sifted, and how and why God works it all out for our good.

Blessedly, God has given us Jesus and the Holy Spirit to bear our problems alongside us and draw us into a deeper faith. While burdened and pained, I've been strengthened spiritually. "God intended it for good to accomplish what is now being done; the saving of many lives" (Gen. 50:20). I've not only survived the sifting, but I'm better for it. That's not pride speaking. That's joy speaking. I'm more patient, grateful, intentional, purposeful, stronger, kinder, and closer to God. It's all too *pala* for me to understand. "Great is the mystery of godliness" (1 Tim. 3:16 ESV).

## SUFFERING ACCELERATES

John Piper said in one of his talks, "The reason that suffering

---

[8] Lewis, C.S. *The Screwtape Letters.* 2016. FAB. Las Vegas, Nevada. (Written July 5, 1941). Page 6.

exists in the universe is so that Christ might display the greatness of the glory of the grace of God in himself as he suffers, by entering into it, suffering himself, that he might by grace deliver us from everlasting suffering."[9]

Everlasting suffering. That's code for hell. And it's not where we want to end up. So, we ask the question; Isn't the kind of suffering which draws us closer to God worth the deliverance of everlasting suffering?

I've seen crisis do one of two things in those around me. It has either led to accelerated faith or accelerated bitterness. Unfortunately, I've witnessed more bitterness than faith. None of us want bitterness to rob us of a joyful life. Jonathan Edwards, theologian from the 1700's, said, "I want to remember these three things: the shortness of life, the suddenness of death, and the length of eternity…always having an eternal perspective because right now counts forever."[10] If you think Jonathan Edwards was a crusty old theologian when he said this, he wasn't. He was seventeen years old, and his eternal lens was already being honed. There's a reason he's known as the greatest revivalist of all time.

God is sovereign. He knows everything that's going to happen to us. He is surprised by nothing. He controls everything. If you and I are to be slobberknockered and tested and tempted over and over, know that it's not for nothing. We are being sifted as wheat so our hard outer shell can fall away, and we can be softened, refined, and made holy.

## FOR A LITTLE WHILE

Our suffering is only for "a little while." Our suffering is not forever, even as it *feels* like forever. Hold onto this promise. Take to heart this godly concept of suffering and time. It will make you more resilient and stronger in your walk with God.

How do we take the truths of the Word and place them in the

---

[9] https://www.desiringgod.org/messages/why-jesus-suffered
[10] https://www.goodreads.com/author/quotes/75887.Jonathan_Edwards

middle of our own hardships? How do we respond in the midst of the sifting?

1.  We decide who Jesus is. Is he the person he says he is? Is he the Savior of your life, and if so, have you given your life over to him?

2.  We fight with a sword. In Matthew 10:34, Jesus says, "I did not come to bring peace, but a sword" (Matthew 10:34). What is the sword? In Ephesians 6, Paul says the sixth piece of armor is "the sword of the Spirit, which is the Word of God" (v. 17). Hebrews 4:12, says, "For the Word of God is alive and active. Sharper than any double–edged sword, it penetrates even to dividing soul and spirit, joints and marrow; it judges the thoughts and attitudes of the heart." Without knowing the Word, we can't control our feelings, rise above our circumstances, or know what God says and how he works.

3.  We practice trust and obedience one step at a time. I've discovered the strength of small and consistent versus big and impulsive. The act of doing anything worthy is not an overnight process. It's a slow crawl. That's ok. The best way I know to crave God and his Word is to do it little by little, every day, until it becomes who you are and what you desire.

4.  We ask God to "stamp eternity on our eyeballs."[11] This is something Jonathan Edwards prayed later in his ministry. This life is not all there is. There's eternal hope of heaven and the promise of a new earth and being with Jesus. It's one of the greatest *pala* of all, the mystery of all mysteries and as such, we struggle to believe it, but once we do, it changes everything.

---

[11] https://www.goodreads.com/author/quotes/75887.Jonathan_Edwards

5.   We recognize that our problems will last only for a little while. Hebrews 10:37, says, "In just a little while, [Jesus] will come and will not delay." We approach life with an eternal lens, and we see today as "a little while." Life, death, and again, life, will happen soon enough.

## MORE OF GOD

Was I being pruned? Was Satan trying to sift the good out of me so I would turn against God? Was the brain tumor the consequence of poor diet and unhealthy living brought upon myself? Is it original sin and the downhill trajectory of the world which will only be resolved with the return of Jesus? Has the journey of a thousand miles of heartache with our youngest daughters turned Mike and I towards God? Is the mystery of it all too much for us to understand? I don't have all the answers, but the beauty is I keep searching for them in God's Word and searching leads me to find more of God and less of me. The other beauty is that I've passed the test because I've not turned away from God. In fact, I am profoundly more surrendered to God. I am closer to God, Jesus, and the Holy Spirit because of my sifting, and I pray I'll continue to survive the sifting. I know it won't be easy. As a believer and a human being, I will be exposed to future heartache, and I pray I survive without succumbing to whatever may come.

## REMEMBER PALA

You don't have to wait to be slobberknockered to understand all of this, but most likely that'll be the way it happens, and when it does, I want you to remember this chapter. I want you to remember *pala* and that it's all too wonderful…too lofty…too extraordinary…too beyond your understanding. I want you to trust that God knows, and then trust in him. Go ahead and "enjoy prosperity while you can, but when hard times strike, realize that both come from God" (Eccles. 7:14 NLT).

Remember, *Jesus will by grace deliver us from everlasting suf-*

*fering,* and one day soon we'll understand. We're going to see our suffering as a prelude to being with Christ and only then will "every tear be wiped away from our eyes, and there will be no more death or mourning or crying or pain, for the old order of things will pass away" (Rev. 21:4), and oh, what a day that will be! Then we'll surely know the marvelous wonder of all that sifting.

# CHAPTER 11

## Study and Reflection

Bible verse: *Jeremiah 29:11* – Read.
Write out in the space below:

_______________________________________________

_______________________________________________

_______________________________________________

_______________________________________________

This verse in Jeremiah 29:11 is one of the most quoted Bible verses of all time. Whole religions have been known to hang their faith on the idea of a God who will prosper those who are devoted and good, and harm those who aren't. Isn't this a core tenet of the prosperity gospel?

How does a chapter on sifting relate to Jeremiah 29:11? Surprisingly, it parallels beautifully with the idea of sifting, and there's no better way to know this than to read. And so, we do. We read. We read. We read some more. We don't throw the whole of the Word out with one-liners and nice platitudes. That's not only a lazy man's faith, it's a wrong faith, an incomplete faith, and perhaps, no faith at all. One verse does not stand alone. That's the beauty, mystery, and complexity of the Bible.

If we read all of Jeremiah 29, we see something very different than a prosperity gospel mentality that Jeremiah 29:11, on its own, leads you to believe. God speaks through the priest and prophet, Jeremiah, to advise the Jews on their present circumstances *of which God has placed them in* (Jer. 29:4 emphasis added). In the KJV it says, "whom I [God] caused to be carried away." What does this sound like to you?

Jeremiah 29 is all about sifting. It's about God's people who God himself banished and exiled. God is imploring them while they are being sifted (exiled) to turn to him. In Jeremiah 29:12-13, God says, "Then you will call on me and come and pray to me and I will listen to you. You will seek me and find me when you seek me with all your heart."

Notice the word *then*. "*Then* you will call on me. *Then* you will come to me. *Then* you will pray to me. *Then* your hearts will seek me." God promises them a plan and a future prosperity. Why? Because God loves his people, and he is a merciful God. He seeks the results of both the sifting and his great mercy.

In the KJV version, you find different language, "For I know the thoughts that I think toward you, saith the LORD, thoughts of peace, and not of evil, to give you an expected end."

God is revealing how he thinks about his people. Thoughts of peace and an expected ending…and ending that's gracious, merciful, hope-filled, and good. When will that happen? At the appointed time. When is that going to be? Well…according to Jeremiah 29, not for a while. In fact, God tells them to settle in for the ride. "Build houses and settle down; plant gardens and eat what they produce. Marry and have sons and daughters; find wives for your sons and give your daughters in marriage, so that they too may have sons and daughters. Increase in number there; do not decrease" (Jer. 29:5–6). How long is this? A long time. Long enough for them to raise children and grandchildren. In fact, in verse 10, God tells them they'll be there for seventy years.

We're so concerned with prospering today; we miss the goal of reaching a better ending. The stories in the Bible are rarely about the here and now, inasmuch as they are about the when and how and of course, about God himself. Jeremiah 29 is God speaking through Jeremiah and God uses first person twenty times. Jeremiah 29 is about God and what God wants, and that's a relationship with his people and he tells them how he's going to accomplish that, and unfortunately (because aren't we all a little hard-headed?), he's going to achieve that through sifting...for their benefit. For their hopeful future.

What about you? Are you going through something painful and difficult to understand? Are you confused to why God would allow hardships in your life? (HINT: God can take your honesty.)

God seeks us, and he often seeks us through sifting, and if that's the case, count it a blessing, even as it feels like (and is) a burden. God purposes to give you an expected ending. Thanks be to God!

> *Lord, your words are more precious than we can fathom, and we ask for a yearning for "the rest of the story" and not pieces and nuggets out of context. We thank you for how you think about us and that you want goodness and peace for our lives. Thank you for our hopeful, holy endings with Jesus. Yet your will be done. Amen.*

# 12

## No Tidy Endings

*One plus one did not equal two. It equaled chaos and heartache.*

His name was Dave,[12] and he was one of Mike's best friends. He was a sweet-natured, soft-spoken, intense man. He was a husband, father, and basketball coach, but above all he was a man who loved Jesus. He had a deep desire for others to know Jesus, and he had a way of making you think about your faith. Really think. You just knew Dave had the ear of God.

He spoke into my heart a year before he would unknowingly face a life-shattering diagnosis, and he asked me one question. It struck a chord, and I've carried it around with me ever since. It was Dave who first made me think seriously about eternity. I was complaining to him about how hard life had become with our two youngest daughters. He listened. Please don't miss this. He listened. He was probably the best listener I've ever known.

He then asked, "Did you ever consider that we aren't meant to be content while we're here on this earth?" One question, but it was the right one for me at the time.

No, I had not considered this. I was young in my Christian walk,

---

[12] This chapter dedicated to Dave Manzer

and I wanted resolutions to my pain. When they didn't come, I was frustrated. One plus one equals two, doesn't it? Isn't that the way it works? Isn't there a logical order to this thing called faith? Believe. Pray. Solution. Believe. Pray. Solution. And on and on it goes. Shouldn't it add up neatly and orderly? After all, Mike and I were clearly led by the Spirit to adopt our daughters. "Whom shall I send? And who will go for us?" was Mike's resounding verse as he prayed and searched the Bible for answers. "And I said, Here I am. Send me!" was his clear answer (Isaiah 6:8). We followed our faith. We did the hard work, yet nothing went as planned. One plus one did not equal two. It equaled chaos and heartache.

Dave's question set me on a different path, one that made me consider not only this life, but the one that comes after this life. Perhaps the chaos in our lives should not be seen as unexpected or unusual. Perhaps it's our expectations which are distorted. Because maybe, just maybe, we are searching for a heaven on earth, one we have no hope of achieving. This is what Dave already understood.

## IT'S ALL SO UNTIDY

We want a world with tidy endings. We want neat packages. We look for understandable outcomes. We are primed early in life for happily ever after. Yet there are no tidy endings on this earth. Death is itself proof of this. We come into this world screaming at birth, and we go out of this world aging into death, or worse yet, we die young, unexpectedly, or in pain. It's all *so* untidy. That's how it's meant to be. That's the sovereignty of God and our destiny. It's original sin, and the witness of the saints, and the history of the world. That's death. And not one of us can escape it.

"Did you ever consider that we are not meant to be content while we're here on this earth?"

When Dave and I spoke in the driveway, he didn't know his life would be shortened. He didn't know his future would soon hold a ten-month battle of illness, prompted by a heart condition from his youth. Nor did he know he would lay in a hospital bed on a kidney machine, waiting for a new heart and a new kidney. He didn't know how abruptly it would all end.

Dave was forty-eight years old when he died. He left behind a wife, two daughters, and a young son. There was still so much fathering to be done. Dave's death isn't unique. There are many cruel deaths and countless others who have died far too young, younger than Dave. His uniqueness was displayed, however, in the way he seemed to know this earth wasn't his home. He knew we aren't meant to achieve the good life here. We're meant to achieve a holy life. We're meant to follow Jesus, love like Jesus loves, disciple others, suffer, and die. I fear you will think me morbid, but if you knew me, you would see I am anything but. There is more life and joy abounding in me than ever before.

## SO CLOSE AND YET...

If you're looking to get to the point in life where your circumstances will be easy or resolved, you may be waiting a long time. You may be waiting until the day you die. Suffering is not always rectified in our lifetime. Read the story of Moses. God says about Moses, "No prophet has risen in Israel like Moses, whom the LORD knew face to face. No one has ever shown the mighty power or performed the awesome deeds that Moses did in the sight of Israel" (Deut. 34:10, 12). If this is true, why does God tell Moses, after forty long difficult years of journeying to the promised land of Canaan that Moses would only "see from a distance the promised land but would never enter the land?" (Deut. 32:52...emphasis added).

As a reader, we journey with Moses through everything he went through, yet God doesn't permit him to *actually* touch the land (the consequence of earlier rebellion). Moses sees the land from a distance but dies without ever entering Canaan. Really? To be so close and yet never reach what he journeyed towards most of his life without resolution seems almost cruel.

No one, other than Jesus, Paul, and perhaps David, gets more airtime than Moses, yet his long journey and deep desire to reach the promised land was never fulfilled. Why? Could it be because the land was not the journey's end? A movie made today would have Moses getting the earthly final prize, yet Moses *did* get the final prize. It just took him forty years to get it because it took him forty years to die. It took him forty years to be with Christ. Suffering and pain have a goal in the life of the believer, and that goal is not the resolution of suffering and pain. It's the person of Jesus.

## OUR CIRCUMSTANCES WILL RESOLVE

Will our circumstances resolve because we follow Christ? Absolutely they will. One day. It just may not be today. Or the next day. Or the one after that. Or in our lifetime. How do we deal with the truth that we may not see our difficult circumstances change in our earthly lifetime? We get up every morning ready to strategize and fight the battle. If we don't, we'll become like I was in my earlier days; defeated and disillusioned. We are not defeated. Jesus has already won the battle for us, and he is forever with us. "We are hard pressed on every side, but not crushed; perplexed, but not in despair; persecuted, but not abandoned; struck down, but not destroyed. We always carry around in our body the death of Jesus, so that the life of Jesus may also be revealed in our body" (2 Cor. 4:8–10).

Joni Eareckson Tada, at seventy-three years old, has served a life-sentence of quadriplegia from a diving accident she had at seventeen. Joni's been preaching the good news of the Gospel ever since, and as if she hasn't suffered enough, she's had Stage III breast cancer, *and* dealt with debilitating pain for more than twenty-five years. I have heard her say on numerous occasions, "I can do quadraplegia, but it's hard to do pain." For over half a century, she's learned to live with one major challenge only to struggle with others. Why must Joni, a willing servant who has moved Christ's kingdom forward, continue to suffer? Could it be for the same reasons my friend, Dave, and Moses suffered? Could it be that contentment and tidy endings on this earth are not our calling? Would we even know Joni Eareckson Tada's name, much less her strong witness for Jesus, without a paralyzing diving accident? Would she be the same strong believer we find today?

## ARE WE READY TO MEET OUR SAVIOR?

I never knew anyone as ready to meet his Savior as Dave was. He wasn't ready to leave his family, nor were they ready to lose him, but he was ready to be with Jesus. I always figured he was too good for this earth. Sometimes you think someone's just not meant to be here any longer. They're meant to go home and be with Jesus.

It's been fifteen years since Dave died, and seventeen years since our moment in the driveway, and yet, I still carry around Dave's simple question as a treasure stored up inside me. There is, as of yet, no resolution with our two youngest daughters. Yet I have faith, trust, patience, and conviction that all will work out as it should. I have more of what the Spirit has grown in me, and more of what Dave had all those years ago. I know now what I didn't know then. We are simply not meant to be content or satisfied in all things earthly, and God will work everything out in his timing, for his good, for our good, and for eternity. Dave was right.

Philippians 3:20–21 says, "Our citizenship is in heaven. And we eagerly await a Savior from there, the Lord Jesus Christ, who, by the power that enables him to bring everything under his control, will transform our lowly bodies so that they will be like his glorious body."

## A NEW KIND OF CONTENTMENT

When Dave got sick, outside of his growing urgency to present the Gospel to whoever he was with, he didn't change. He didn't despair. He didn't waver in his faith. He battled his illness and grew in his desire to reach others for Jesus. And like Paul, in his writings through his many struggles, I never saw an ounce of self-pity in Dave.

Dave was the epitome of Philippians 4:11–12, when Paul tells us, "I have learned to be content whatever the circumstances. I know what it is to be in need, and I know what it is to have plenty. I have learned the secret of being content in any and every situation, whether well fed or hungry, whether living in plenty or in want. I can do all this through him who gives me strength."

Jesus told his disciples, "Now is your time of grief, but I will see you again and you will rejoice, and no one will take away your joy" (John 16:22), and then he told them, "In this world you will have trouble. But take heart! I have overcome the world" (John 16:33).

A key question for us to consider as we work through the downs of life is this: Will our difficult, fearful, or debilitating circumstances work themselves out? Yes. One day. It may not be today. Or the next day. Or the one after that. Or in our lifetime. And yet we are not defeated. Jesus has overcome the world. God is with us. He asks for our trust.

Jesus is the Prince of peace, the Word incarnate, our Interceder, our Mediator, and our Savior. One day, when we're in heaven with him, we will finally have what we can't possibly have here on this earth, as Dave so wisely pointed out to me. The challenge is for us to grasp this truth, hold on tightly to God's promises, especially in times that are so hard we don't know how to get through them. Hold on we must, because one day we'll go out of this world and into the next, and we'll finally have our tidy endings. "Lay up the treasures of God as your firm foundation for the coming age, so that they may take hold of the life that is truly life" (1 Tim. 6:19). When we do this, we'll know what Dave knew seventeen years ago, and what he continues to know today, and we'll finally be content. Truly content.

# CHAPTER 12

Bible verse: *Deuteronomy 34* – Read the chapter.
Write out verse 4a in the space below:

_________________________________________

_________________________________________

_________________________________________

_________________________________________

Abraham. Isaac. Jacob. Moses. Joshua. These are men who understood the value of passing something on to their descendants. They understood the importance of genealogy. They acted on behalf of the generations that came before them and the generations who would come after them.

As I am in my sixties, I find genealogy relevant in a way I didn't in my younger years, but my desire is for all to know this relevancy sooner than I did. The quicker we see the powerful effect our lives have on others, the more effective we will be in and for the kingdom. The quicker we see this is the quicker we can know that tidy endings may not happen in our lifetime. We see a higher purpose and know that our "real" promised land is with Jesus.

God's people, Moses included, had a lot of issues. They were sinners like you and me. They deserved nothing from God. And yet, God gave them so much. Moses, by God's mercy and grace, got to see the land of Canaan. God kept his promise, and not only his promise to Moses, but to the descendants of Abraham.

Deuteronomy 34:9 has a promising sentence in it regarding Joshua, Moses' successor, "So the Israelites listened to him [Joshua] and did what the LORD had commanded Moses." Moses had just died and finally, the Israelites were allowed to enter Canaan. Finally, they were going to get the rest they needed. Finally, they did what the LORD commanded them to do.

We are not always privy to tidy endings, but God keeps his promises. If you are saved by the blood of Jesus, you are promised a good ending. Perhaps it takes age and maturity and/or a crisis to see death as an imminent reality. And yet, I'm hopeful that the young will stop to consider their ending *and* their impact on others.

What stops you from being content in the Lord now?

What stops you from believing God's promises in the midst of hardship?

We may not always have outcomes revealed to us (like Moses did), but nonetheless, we can trust God for them. You can rest in and be content that he will bring his goodness to pass. We can trust in God's promises.

What are some "godly" promises worth relying on?

> *Lord, your promises can be trusted…for us and for our children and their children and those we care about reaching for Jesus…and so forth and so forth. Abraham. Isaac. Jacob. Moses. Joshua. Our heroes in the faith weren't perfect, yet they all had one thing in common. They reached the real promised land, the one with Jesus. Let us be so blessed to be added to their names in the same way. Yet your will be done. Amen.*

# THE CHALLENGE OF CULTURE

*"You were running a good race. Who cut in on you to keep you from obeying the truth? That kind of persuasion does not come from the one who calls you. A little yeast works through the whole batch of dough."*
Galatians 5:9

# 13

## *Flee For Your Life*

*How many of us would have been able to keep from turning back?*

I had a career, and it was a good one. It contributed to a healthy household income, and more importantly, it gave me a positive outlet and purpose away from a home filled with challenges. Mike often called my busy career a "24/7 lifestyle," which probably helped forgive its constant interruptions. I was good at what I did, and I loved my team of four, which included Sarah. I loved the hundreds of people I met along the way. It was such a good fit for me, I used to say I was born to it. Until a brain tumor came along and showed me something different. What I thought was important became unimportant, and a year after the tumor's removal, my first granddaughter Nora arrived, putting a pink bow on the gift of an ordained slowdown. Without the tumor and without grandchildren, I can say with one-hundred percent certainty, I'd never have left my career. I'd still be running like a hamster, spinning on the wheels of a solid, good, self-affirming business. Spinning…spinning…sometimes out of control…sometimes nice and steady…sometimes with joy…sometimes with stress…but always spinning.

My passion for real estate ended when *better* passions took over. It became more valuable to live intentionally for family and be purposeful for Jesus with the years I had left. The God-ordained slowdown helped me see what I couldn't see on my own and once I left, I never looked back. I never thought about the business of real estate again.

Success, busyness, position, money, and fame are culture's affirmation of a worthy and admirable life, but they can lure us away from a strong and purposeful walk with God. What culture esteems is what Satan uses as an inroad to "steal, kill, and destroy," or at a minimum, distract and dissuade. You might think I'm being dramatic, but if you are caught unaware (like I was), you'll find yourself at culture's mercy, because what looks admirable is not what God considers admirable. We want to keep our eye on the prize of Jesus and what he has come to do, "give us life to the full" (John 10:10 paraphrased).

## THE APPEARANCE OF BENIGN

When the brain tumor was discovered, we all breathed a sigh of relief for the benign diagnosis. I felt like I dodged a bullet when we found out it wasn't cancer, but quickly discovered that benign doesn't mean unimpactful. The gamma knife radiation treatment led to swelling on the brain and swelling led to partial paralysis on the left side of my body. At my worst, I couldn't move on my own or be left alone. I needed assistance getting out of a chair or bed. Walking a short distance became an event. When I was walking, I couldn't be distracted. If someone tried to talk to me, I couldn't engage. I literally couldn't walk and chew gum at the same time. I forgot basic words and my thoughts were unclear. My emotions were exaggerated as I became easily overwhelmed, sometimes crying over nothing. Every physical, mental, and emotional part of me was negatively impacted.

When we finally found a neurosurgeon to remove the tumor, he didn't mince words when he said, "You could be paralyzed for the rest of your life if it doesn't come out immediately." Paralyzed for the rest of my life. It was daunting and scary, and that benign tumor was anything but benign.

I view culture in the same way. Nothing is benign. All of it seeks to capture our attention and our hearts. I'm not going to specifically point out culture's potential traps. They vary from place to place, and person to person, nor would it be proper for me to make a list of right and wrong for anyone to follow. That's a slippery slope to legalism and not at all the message of my heart.

That said, there are attitudes or characteristics of culture which threaten a strong walk of faith. If we evaluate everything through the lens of Scripture, we undoubtedly see that what culture values will not align with the truths of the Word. Consider worldly buzzwords like acceptance, independence, choice, individualism, equality, privacy, authenticity, inclusion, personal rights, and so forth. I could go on and I'm sure you can come up with others. View each of these attitudes through God's Word, and you will see how they are corrupted. Even seemingly good ideas like love and forgiveness can become corrupt if not viewed through biblical truth.

## IF IT FEELS RIGHT

I overheard a discussion recently about making decisions on the basis of whether something feels right or not. A woman was asked the question, "How do you know what's right or wrong." The answer? "You just know deep within yourself."

This attitude is commonplace. "You just know," or "if it feels right, you should do it" are two prevailing thoughts many of us have, and they claim that by some internal meter we can determine what is right and wrong. This is a pervasive lie, and according to the Word, we cannot determine what is right or wrong. What we think "feels right" may not be biblically sound. Our inner gauge isn't the proper gauge and following the Bible isn't natural. It's countercultural, counterintuitive, and counterproductive to living a holy godly life.

## NO HELL FOR ANYONE

You might have heard it said, "If God is a loving God, how can he send anyone to hell?" Neither the Old nor the New Testament teaches about a God who is incapable of bringing down justice on those who do not know and obey him, yet our culture believes it, and because they do, they trivialize the need to be saved by Jesus Christ, repent of sins, know the Word, and live up to a worthy faith. Our culture trivializes Hell, either thinking it a fairy tale, or God doesn't have it in him to send anyone there.

2nd Thessalonians 1:8–9 says, "He [God] will punish those who do not know God and do not obey the gospel of our Lord Jesus. They will be punished with everlasting destruction and shut out from the presence of the Lord and from the glory of his might." Who will go to Hell? Those who "do not know God" and who "do not obey the gospel."

## CHOSEN AND CALLED

Chosen and called are misunderstood terms, even within Christian circles. The Word says God is patient and waits for all to be saved, and yet, it also says not everyone will be called. Jesus says in Matthew 22:14, "For many are invited [called], but few are chosen." Jesus doesn't say *all* are invited, nor does he say *all* are chosen. He doesn't even say many or most are chosen. He says *few* are chosen. It's not easy to understand, yet revelation comes with reading the Bible. The Spirit gives understanding, so we are made less *self*-aware and more *God*-aware.

"None of us are as self-aware as we think we are," Mike said to me recently. I've taken this statement to heart. I'm not as self-aware as I think I am. None of us are. I want to be both self-aware and God-aware.

## SHE TURNED HER NECK

Genesis 19 tells the story of Lot and his wife, known only as "Lot's wife." Lot is told by two men (who were angels), "Get them (Lot's family) out of here, because we are going to destroy this place" (Gen. 19:12, 13). God is preparing to destroy the wicked city of Sodom, along with the city of Gomorrah, and through his mercy, decides to save Lot and his family (because of Abraham – Gen. 19:29).

So, Lot and his family, in their strong belief and distress, listened to the men immediately, and dropped everything and ran.

NOT.

Lot and his wife did *not* drop everything and run. They hesitated, and when they did, "the men [angels] grasped Lot's hand, the hands of his wife, and two daughters, and led them safely out of the city, for the LORD was merciful to them" (Gen. 19:16). The angels say to them, "Flee for your lives! Don't look back, and don't stop anywhere in the plain! Flee to the mountains or you will be swept away!" (Gen. 19:17).

Being literally dragged to safety, the family traveled to the next town, and we read, "But Lot's wife looked back, and she became a pillar of salt" (19:26). It doesn't say why she looked back. It doesn't say anything about the condition of her heart. It doesn't say she looked back longingly or sorrowfully or regretfully or wistfully. It just says, "she looked back."

Such a simple directive from God to Lot's family, it's easy to be overlooked. "Don't look back." Let's be honest here. What did Lot's wife do that was so horrible to gain the wrath and justice of God in such a way? How many of us would have been able to keep from turning back? The way we strain our necks on the highway as we pass a serious accident. The way we stay tuned to a screaming child melting down in a store. They way we are captivated by a scene we know we shouldn't be watching on TV. The sensational is…well… sensational. Captivating. Consuming. Drawing. It beckons to us to turn towards it and seek it out.

What about Lot? How was Lot's wife worse than Lot having to be dragged out? He didn't seem too keen on leaving Sin City either. And yet it was his wife who was destroyed, to be forever nameless, nothing more than a pillar of salty disobedience.

I don't know the *wonder* of it all, but I've considered this story because the demise of Lot's wife is a powerful example of our propensity to not take God and his Word as, pardon the pun, gospel. We find Lot's wife mentioned again in Luke 17:33, which gives us a clue to the condition of her heart, "Remember Lot's wife! Whoever tries to keep their life will lose it." We now see the truth which had not been revealed in Genesis. Lot's wife wanted to be *in* the life she was told to leave. She wanted to stay in Sin City. She didn't want to leave. Her neck turned because her heart was left behind, and God knew full well the condition of her heart.

We live in a different time and place, and yet, our culture's similarities to Sodom and Gomorrah are chilling. It threatens to captivate our hearts in the same way Sodom captivated Lot and his family. I see it in myself and my past career. I was saved. I was a believer, yet there were parts of my career which promoted the turning of my neck away from God. I was successful to the point of not seeing my need of God. I didn't take the time to think about him. I didn't take time for Bible study. I didn't take time for church activities. I was too busy to be involved. A fruitful and purposeful career gave to me, but it also took from me, and I allowed it to take from me.

"My heart took delight in all my labor, and this was the reward for all my toil. Yet when I surveyed all that my hands had done and what I had toiled to achieve, everything was meaningless, a chasing after the wind; nothing was gained under the sun" (Eccles. 2:10–11).

When I "set my face like a flint" (Isaiah 50:7), read, and take the Word to heart, and seek God and the Spirit's guidance in my life, I started to walk the walk God meant for me to walk. And when I did, the distractions of a much-too-busy career and worldly success weakened their grip on me.

## JESUS AT THE FOREFRONT

How do we honor toil and hard work, a successful career, a busy family, our passions for good things (like nutrition, exercise, writing, and speaking) and not let them captivate our hearts away from godliness? How do we protect the inroads Satan is so good at finding, even in those things designated as "good things?"

We take Jesus out of the peripheral of our lives and put him in the forefront. We wake up every morning with the thought of what he did for us, who he is to us, and seek wisdom which only comes from Scripture. We ask the Holy Spirit for guidance, and we respond when he prompts us, even if that prompting (or opportunity) is something counter to what we want or think we should do. Even if it's risky.

We run God's race, not our own race, and we run with courage, without shame, trusting the Word in us. God hasn't changed. We have. God's directives are the same for us as they were for those found on the pages of the Old and New Testament. We have Jesus, who paid the price for our sins, and who came to fulfill the law, not diminish or change it.

"How then can we live? We should turn from our evil ways and live" (Ezk. 33:10–11…emphasis added). We're told we must lose this life in favor of God's life. How do we do this? Here are a few guiding principles to consider (you can add your own as well):

1. Believe — "The message of the cross is foolishness to those who are perishing, but to us who are being saved it is the power of God" (1 Cor. 1:18).

2. Read — "Sanctify them by the truth; your word is truth" (John 17:17).

3. Pray — "Show me your ways LORD. Teach me your paths" (Psalm 25:4).

4. Trust — "In the LORD my God, I put my trust" (Psalm 25:1).

5. Guard — "Be alert and of sober minded. Your enemy the devil prowls around like a roaring lion looking for someone to devour" (1 Peter 5:8).

6. Stand — "…stand your ground" (Eph. 6:13).

7. Endure — "Let us lay aside every encumbrance and the sin which so easily entangles us, and let us run with endurance the race that is set before us, fixing our eyes on Jesus, the author and perfecter of faith, who for the joy set before Him endured the cross, despising the shame, and has sat down at the right hand of the throne of God" (Heb. 12:1–2).

## NEW(ER) CREATION

I'm still becoming new(er) in Christ. I've discovered the journey of a strong faith walk leads to an ongoing newness in Christ and the Word. We are first made new when we accept Jesus as our Savior. "Therefore, if anyone is in Christ, the new creation has come: The old has gone, the new is here" (2 Cor. 5:17). There's an ongoing newness to a growing faith journey. There's a fancy name for it called sanctification, which means the process of becoming purified and holy. It's the work of the Spirit in our lives, our response to him, and a growing knowledge and joy in Jesus which doesn't stop throughout our lifetime.

There's a reason Jesus and the Spirit are continually at work in us. We need them. We can't do it on our own. I'm grateful Jesus doesn't stop interceding for me. The Spirit doesn't stop moving and guiding my thoughts and actions. And, God the Father, doesn't stop cherishing me. The triune God, a mystery I'll never quite grasp, is who we can trust to be in our corner, more than we can be in our own corner. Like a small child who doesn't know what's best for him, we don't know what's best for us. We can't do whatever *feels* right because the world's right is not God's right.

I don't want to be like Lot's wife. I don't want to turn and look back, desiring the ways of the world which can be so darn appealing. Do we really need to "flee for our lives"? Does it have to be so radical? Isn't a little moderation just what the doctor ordered? Nope. Not even close.

# CHAPTER 13

## Study and Reflection

Bible verse: *Genesis 19* – Read the chapter.
Write out verse 19:19b in the space below:

_______________________________________

_______________________________________

_______________________________________

_______________________________________

I find the story of Lot and his wife (and family) in Genesis 19 to be a fascinating one. As we reflect on how this chapter relates to our lives, I can't help but draw near to three little words. They are in the middle of verse 19 (NIV). They are revealing, relatable, and worthy of our attention.

But. I. Can't.

It's not the only time we find these kinds of words in Scripture. Moses said them to God when he said, "Please send someone else" (Ex. 4:13). Jeremiah said them (Jer. 1:6), "I am too young." Jonah said them (by his actions), "But Jonah ran away from the Lord" (Jonah 1:3). And Peter clearly showed his weakness when he denied being a disciple of Jesus to a servant girl, "I am not" (John 18:17).

But. I. Can't.

In *Strong, From Here to Eternity*, I write about risk and reward. Among the things I said was, "We want to risk only as much as we're willing to give, and truthfully, for me, that can be very little," and,

"The problem [with this kind of risk] is that we hold ourselves closer than the God of the universe."[13]

But. I. Can't.

Why do we say we can't or won't? Why do we run away from the call of God and the truths of his Word?

What will it cost us if we follow God?

It's going to cost us time, effort, comfort, status, pride, etc. God tells us it will cost us our lives. We can no more remove the cost of following Jesus within our walk of faith, than we can remove the sin of not following him.

Matthew 16:26 asks us, "For what will it profit a man if he gains the whole world and forfeits his soul?" (ESV).

The next time you hear a nudge of the Spirit, a call on your heart, a clear leading from God into a place that's going to cost you something, even if it's something as little as helping someone in the grocery store, or turning off an inappropriate TV program, I urge you to listen. Jesus says, (John 18:37), "Everyone on the side of truth listens to me." Jesus came to save us from our wretched state, and it's good and desirable and game-changing to listen when he calls. We no longer need to say, "But, I can't."

I'm reminded of the lyrics to a favorite childhood song. Let this be our prayer today.

*I have decided to follow Jesus;*
*No turning back, no turning back.*
*The world behind me, the cross before me;*
*No turning back, no turning back.*
*Though none go with me, still I will follow;*
*No turning back, no turning back.*
*My cross I'll carry, till I see Jesus;*
*No turning back, no turning back.*
*Will you decide now to follow Jesus?*
*No turning back, no turning back.*[14]
*Amen.*

---

[13] Walker, Sheri. *Strong, From Here to Eternity*. Page 69.
[14] https://library.timelesstruths.org/music/I_Have_Decided_to_Follow_Jesus/

# 14

# An Un-Moderate Life

*I was the frog. I was boiling and had no idea.*

More than twenty years ago, I saw a movie so disturbing, the images stayed with me for years afterwards. Those images are now successfully behind me, but I had to work at training my thoughts to go in a different direction every time they resurfaced. If I saw the movie's title flash on the TV listing guide, I quickened my finger on the remote to hurry past it. It took redirection and lots of time to stop those disturbing images from taking over. I can write about it here without any recall. There's no doubt God has helped me with this selective memory loss.

Two short hours of my life not only corrupted and disturbed me but took a long time to get out of my system. Who knows if it will ever be completely gone from the depths of me. It taught me something about what I let in. To this day, Mike will tell you how soft I am with TV selections. If it's not G (ok, some PG), I rarely indulge. Even at sixty-one, I'm highly impressionable. I avoid all things violent, scary, evil, sexualized, distasteful, and voyeuristic which means, unfortunately, I find most programming inappropriate. You'd find me watching Alaska shows, Heartland, Christian or family movies, and veterinary shows before you'd find me watching anything else.

The older I get, the less tolerant I am with programming not deemed appropriate for most five-year olds.

## THE FROG IN THE KETTLE

As the fable goes, if you put a frog in a boiling pot, upon feeling the heat, he quickly jumps out saving himself from sure death. However, if you put a frog in a cool pot of water and slowly bring the water to a boil one degree at a time, he never perceives the danger until it's too late, ultimately boiling him to death.

The same can be said of the choices we make. That disturbing movie was like a big dose of hot water on my soul. Yet it's often not one choice that hurts us, in the same way it's not one drop of boiling water that kills the frog. It's the slow and steady cumulative drops which eventually boil us to death.

When it came to my physical and spiritual health, I was the frog. For much of my adult life, I was coming to a slow boil and had no idea. There were indulgences I was unwilling to know because I was unwilling to change. I didn't want to give up the comfort, the food, the career, and the lifestyle, which on one level or another became over-indulgent and harmful. When it came to my health for instance, it took a lot of drops to find me at a place of illness, and it was going to take a complete mind shift to get me out of that pot and into safety.

Human nature is such that we don't stop at a drop. We blame our choices on being moderate, until the very moderation we see as acceptable is the one which ends up hurting us; one piece of cake at a time, one bad movie at a time, one nasty word to a spouse at a time, one indulgence, decision, or sinful choice at a time. Before you know it, the choices we make are boiling us. We so often don't perceive the danger until it's too late. Moderation is a persuasive inroad to deceive us away from holiness.

## IN "CAHOOTS"

Through the most difficult teenage years with our youngest daughters, Mike would come home from work at the end of the day, and I'd unload on him, "They were awful today," or "I can't take it anymore," or "I'm done." He'd agree with me, and we'd commiserate together. We were one cohesive complaining bad-mouthing team because it felt good to vent. Unfortunately, our adversaries happened to be our daughters. And although Mike and I were unified with each other, we started to recognize our pattern was harmful. Our words were poisonous, and were infecting our attitudes, and if we were to promote healthy relationships with our girls, what *felt* good had to be stopped. We recognized the drips of wrong. We stopped our bad-mouthing and became accountable to each other in what we said and how we said it. It didn't mean we couldn't vent on occasion or be honest, but we stopped pitting ourselves against our daughters, and we made ourselves see their pain, not just our own. We kept each other grounded to build up, not tear down. Although our bashing was never in front of our girls, it didn't matter. They knew.

Once we stopped the bad-mouthing, we vented in healthier ways, and tried to find solutions to encourage growth in all of us, especially compassion within our hearts. We didn't always succeed, and I still don't always succeed, but it made us aware and changed us for the better. Right was right and wrong was wrong, and it took Mike (I'm sorry to say it wasn't me) to step up and say "this is wrong" before we made concrete changes.

No one was going to arrest us for trash-talking our teenagers behind their backs, but it wasn't beneficial or constructive for any of us. It was undoubtedly a slippery slope away from holiness. A little wrong never makes a right.

## THE DRIPS OF MODERATION

It's easy for us to buy into the "everything in moderation" theory. A culture of moderation has, in some ways, replaced God's Word. We don't see how far gone we are. The practice of everything in moderation protects us from being offensive, and of course, we are *very* careful not to offend anyone. The social sin of offending for lack of being accepting seems to supersede everything else, including truth, purity, righteousness, and godliness.

Everything in moderation is lauded, encouraged, and promoted in our culture in almost everything we do. Could it be an excuse? An excuse not to try? An excuse to lean towards indulgence without guilt? An excuse to explain away bad behavior? An excuse not to look stupid and awkward? The Word and the world are diametrically opposed, and as Christians hoping to walk in a strong faith, we need to live in strong truth, even when we look like an outcast.

## WHAT'S MODERATE ANYWAY?

The *I love Lucy* show ran for six seasons, from 1951–1957, and was considered by many to be scandalous. Although Lucy and Desi were married in real life *and* on their TV show, they weren't allowed to be shown in bed or have even a hint of sexual intimacy. The real scandal, however, was when Lucille Ball became pregnant. The network hid her pregnancy in season one. They weren't allowed to say the word pregnant. *The Code of Practices for Television Broadcasters* prohibited anything sexually suggestive on the air, including the discussion of pregnancy (or the word), since it implied that a couple, even a married one, had engaged in sex.

In today's world, this seems ridiculous, but consider how far we've come. Consider the drips. What was done in 1950 would have been unheard of in 1900. And what was scandalous in 1950 seems ridiculous today, and what is scandalous now will seem ridiculous fifty years from now. Consider the most popular shows on any streaming service. I can't even gaze on the titles or pictures associated with many of the shows, much less open them for viewing. They are not just distasteful. They're downright evil.

Have we gone too far? Who dictates too far gone anyway? What is the tipping point, the one that finds us being boiled, and will we recognize it? Have we already been boiled?

Can we fit a moderate life into biblical truth, or does biblical truth have to override our cultural idea of moderation? And, if the latter, are we going to look foolish when we commit, really commit, to following the Word of God, even within our family and friend circles? Are we going to be *that* person, the Jesus freak?

Let's get one thing straight. If you believe the inerrancy of the Bible, then you must believe it's the same Word of God whether you were born in the 1600's or 2024. Scripture is not the thing that changes. "The grass withers and the flowers fall, but the Word of our God endures forever" (Isaiah 40:8). "Your word, LORD, is eternal; it stands firm in the heavens." (Psalm 119:89). Because of this truth, it doesn't matter when you were born. Culture can't be the dictator of our choices and who we are in Christ. Is all this talk just a good ole dose of legalism? God's grace is going to cover us anyway, right? Don't be deceived into thinking what we do doesn't matter, and Jesus' death on the cross doesn't need to impact our behaviors. I don't want to be at the end of *that* judgement.

## AN UN-MODERATE JESUS

As I pondered the lives of people I admire — Fred Rogers, Corrie Ten Boom, Jim and Elisabeth Elliot, Amy Carmichael, Noah, the Apostle Paul — I couldn't find moderation in any of them.

Then there's Jesus. Jesus wasn't a moderate nor is there anything moderate about Scripture and its messages. Jesus said, as is recorded in John 15:5, "I am the vine; you are the branches. If you remain in me and I in you, you will bear much fruit; apart from me you can do nothing." Nothing. Jesus spoke like this all the time. He didn't say, apart from me you can do some things, or even a few things. He said you can do *nothing*. Jesus' teachings were strong, unambiguous, and while filled with love and grace, they certainly weren't moderate. He wasn't preaching moderation. He was preaching (as does the entire Bible) an all or nothing faith. And of course, there's nothing moderate about the cross Jesus died a cruel death on. He went all in to save you and me from our sins.

## MODERATION DIDN'T CHANGE MY HEALTH

Seven years ago, finding myself in such poor shape, I had to take charge of my health. I lost almost a third of my body weight, and despite being told by doctors that high cholesterol and high blood pressure were "familial" and controllable only with medication, I was able to bring my levels to normal and get off all medication. Other conditions supposedly here to stay, like arthritis in my hands, headaches, and sinus issues, have all disappeared. I couldn't have achieved this by being moderate. I did it through effort, denial, education, and a commitment to good daily choices and habits. I've found I'm unable to slide back into a more moderate lifestyle. Moderation puts weight back on, inflames and weakens my body, and gives me pain and adverse side-effects. I've learned that moderation, as much as I'd like it to, will not keep me healthy. Am I always perfect? Of course not, but I pay for the slip-ups, and they are good reminders of my big why, as they prompt me to stay the course, as un-moderate as it sometimes feels or appears.

## SATAN LOVES MODERATION

Moderation is a deceiver. It deceives you into thinking a little bit is ok because after all, it's just a little bit. What's the big deal? Satan doesn't appear to us like the devil, scaring us with fangs and an ugly appearance. He comes slyly and one of the ways he comes is in the form of moderation. He says it's no big deal. Everyone's doing it. One bad movie. A little catty talk. One extra glass of wine. A little deceit. A little sex in a movie. One little drop. No big deal.

Sin is most deceptive when it's subtle. Sin whispers to you that a little indulgence and wickedness is not bad, and in fact, it's just harmless fun. This is the slippery slope, the frog in the kettle, the slow drips of corruption, even the ones we consider harmless and are culturally widely accepted. Don't be deceived. They are taking your soul one drop at a time. Which drop will be the one that pushes you over the edge? Which will be the one that keeps you indulging deeper and deeper, going further and further. Will you know?

## ASK THE RIGHT QUESTION

Is what I'm doing moving me away from God or towards him? I ask myself this question often. I want to be closer to God, closer to his truths, and closer to bringing others to know him, especially through godly example. That's a discerning life of stewardship and holiness.

If you shun moderation for the slippery slope it is, it will be uncomfortable. Most of us don't like to be uncomfortable. I'm a pleaser by nature, and I don't want anyone to feel uncomfortable by my decisions not to partake in something I find less than honorable. Dissention isn't comfortable, yet the Word predicts our discomfort of being "unacceptable" to others. In John 15:18–19, Jesus says, "If the world hates you, keep in mind that it hated me first. If you belonged to the world, it would love you as its own. As it is, you do not belong to the world, but I have chosen you out of the world. That is why the world hates you." If we are to settle into a strong faith, we'd better get used to being unacceptable by some and disliked or even hated by others.

As we train for godliness, we'll see the "normal" drips of moderation for what they are and that's sin. How do we prevent the drips? Go back one chapter and read my seven guiding principles again. They are to help us recognize and defeat the threats to our faith as we move forward in a stronger walk with God.

I want to add to my list:

8. Eternity — "That whoever believes in him shall not perish but have eternal life" (John 3:16). Eternal hope of being with Jesus helps you fight the battle. Stay the course. Keep on keeping on. Know that this life is not the end.

## KNOW JESUS

The Bible is the filter for what's right and wrong, holy and unholy, and the more you dive in, the less blurry the lines will be. Holiness takes hold of your heart more than the world's call, and you will pull away from things which don't align with God. I encourage you to strive, not specifically for an un-moderate life, but one committed to live for Jesus. Once you do, the drips of a moderate culture will become undesirable. They will dissipate and dry up, as the pouring of the Spirit comes upon you and gives you strength. Eventually, you'll worry less about being an outlier, an outcast, or a Jesus-freak because you'll see there's nothing better than being an un-moderate freak for Jesus.

# CHAPTER 14

## Study and Reflection

Bible verse: *Matthew 3* – Read all.
Write out verse 2 in the space below:

_______________________________________________

_______________________________________________

_______________________________________________

_______________________________________________

I don't know too many people who relate to John the Baptist. He's not someone we think to emulate. "John's clothes were made of camel's hair, and he had a leather belt around his waist. His food was locusts and wild honey" (Matt. 3:4). He called people to repent, and he wasn't afraid to call out those in power, "You brood of vipers!" (v. 3:7), and "produce fruit in keeping with repentance" (v. 3:8).

We are told, before John's birth, that he would be a "joy and delight" to his parents, and that "he will be great in the sight of the Lord. He is never to take wine or other fermented drink, and he will be filled with the Holy Spirit even before he is born" (Luke 1:14-15). In Luke 1:80, it says, "And the child [John] grew and became strong in spirit; and he lived in the wilderness until he appeared publicly to Israel."

John, from childhood, lived in the wilderness. He was removed from society. Isolated. Untainted, if you will. He ate locusts and wild honey. Wild honey. That's not honey poured nicely out of a jar. He got it directly from the bees' nest. I bet he was stung a few [hundred] times. We are told that John is "A voice of one calling in the wilderness 'Prepare the way for the Lord, make straight paths for him'" (Matt. 3:3).

This is how God chooses to announce the Messiah of the world; with a wild man, isolated most of his life, separated from society.

Honestly, I can't imagine being anything like John the Baptist. I'm fairly proper. I shower and do my makeup every day, even if I'm home by myself. I have a schedule and the older I get, the more fastidious I become. I'm careful with my words, my actions, my dress, and my life. The whole idea of being a "John the Baptist" is not only unappealing, but a bit horrifying. I have enough trouble (in public) waving my hands in the air to a moving worship song. I'm a bit inward with my feelings. Simply put, I probably won't be yelling at anyone anytime soon to "repent of their sins."

I love Jesus, but am I sold out for him? Are you? What does that even look like?

I can't answer the question for you. I can only answer it for me, and I'll admit that I am nowhere close to the "sold out" passion of John the Baptist. What is true is that I'm moving towards a close, intimate, relationship to God, His Son, and the Holy Spirit, and what that looks like for me is time. Time spent with Jesus. Time spent in the Word, in prayer, in communion, in listening to and being with a community of pastors, believers, and witnesses. Time spent learning about people like John the Baptist.

I don't think I'll ever be anything like John the Baptist, and that's ok. I'm like Sheri Walker, just like you're like _______________________ [fill in the blank].

Living a life that's sold out for Jesus has to start with you selling out. Selling out the world for the Word; you for God; and selling out a life spent in fear and comfort to one spent in courage and service. That happens little by little with the gradual, ongoing sanctification of a life being perfected in Christ.

The last words we hear from John the Baptist are found in John 3:36. He says, "Whoever believes in the Son has eternal life, but whoever rejects the Son will not see life, for God's wrath remains on them."

There's nothing moderate about John the Baptist, as he prepared his whole life to announce the Messiah. And there's nothing moderate about Jesus. He is the Alpha and the Omega, the First and the Last, the Beginning and the End…the Root and the Offspring of David, and the bright Morning Star" (Rev. 22:13, 16). Amen and amen.

> *Lord, you are the I Am. The first and the last. Help us to be sold out to and for you, like our great witness, John the Baptist, was. Help us to overcome fear and take on the courage of the Spirit within us. Yet your will be done. Amen.*

# FINAL CHALLENGES

*"Though the fig tree does not bud and there are no grapes on the vines,*
*though the olive crop fails, and the fields produce no food,*
*though there are no sheep in the pen and no cattle in the stalls,*
*yet I will rejoice in the* Lord, *I will be joyful in God my Savior.*
*The sovereign* Lord *is my strength."*
Habakkuk 3:17–19

# 15

*Honey, are you born of the Spirit?*

I accepted Jesus when I was a young teenager at summer Bible camp. Through my church, summer camps, and my paternal grandparents, I received a basic foundation in who Jesus is and what it means to follow him. What I didn't get clear teaching on was the Holy Spirit. That was ok with me as I was content to steer clear of him. The only people I knew who spoke about the Holy Spirit were a few overzealous relatives who claimed to speak in tongues. I wanted nothing to do with their weird religious practices.

Two of those relatives cornered me one summer day when we were at a family gathering and asked, "Honey, are you born of the Spirit?" Not wanting to look like a heathen, I said, "Yes, I am." We all gave each other a knowing grin, and then I inched away from them as fast as I could. Their question made me so uncomfortable. I didn't know what they were talking about. To this day, I don't know who those relatives were, yet vividly remember the question and the embarrassment I felt. The incident made me cautious about how I talk to others about God, yet I now understand their question, and because I do, I'd like to hereby offer a formal apology for thinking my relatives wacky. For the record, I have now become the wacky relative.

Back then, I didn't understand who the Holy Spirit is, what he does, and how he fits into a saving relationship with Jesus. I didn't know the Holy Spirit himself gives understanding. "The person without the Spirit does not accept the things that come from the Spirit of God but considers them foolishness and cannot understand them because they are discerned only through the Spirit" (1 Cor. 2:14). Isn't it remarkable that it's because of the Holy Spirit we understand who the Spirit is *and* who God is?

The Holy Spirit is so often the forgotten one. The discredited one. The odd one out. The one we don't talk about. Why? Because we don't understand. There's enough mystery within our walk with God but the Spirit is the biggest mystery of all. A faceless hovering Spirit, from the beginning of Genesis to the end of Revelation.

The person of the Holy Spirit was for me, the last person of the triune God whom I recognized and invited into my life. Don't get me wrong. He was already there. I was sealed with the Spirit when I asked Jesus into my heart. I just never gave him his full due. But not anymore. I want to, as John MacArthur says, "Restore the rightful place of the Holy Spirit in the Christian church.[15]" The Holy Spirit is our great gift. I'm still learning who he is and how great his impact is. I'm sorry I discredited the Spirit early on, but I'm making up for lost time as I learn, listen, love, pray, and seek him. And I'd love to invite you into this powerful relationship with the Holy Spirit as a part of your walk with all three of the triune God given to us.

## OUR SUPERMAN CAPE

Jesus said to the disciples, "I am going to send you what my Father has promised; but stay in the city until you have been clothed with power from on high" (Luke 24:49). The ESV translation says, "I [Jesus] am sending the promise." What is the promise? The Holy

---

[15]   https://www.gty.org/library/sermons-library/CONF-SC12-03/reclaiming-the-worship-of-the-holy-spirit

Spirit. Jesus told them to stay in the city *until* they have been *clothed with power.*" What does Jesus mean when he says they will be clothed with power?

Is it like Clark Kent, whose cape gives him additional powers? Clark puts on his cape, and he's transformed into Superman with supernatural powers. A google search reveals certain characteristics about Superman's cape. It provided him with added protection, acting as a shield, and was also used to carry and rescue people. And it was indestructible. I love this imagery. Clark Kent puts on the cape, and it transforms him into all he can be in his role of Superman.

Is this what the power of the Holy Spirit is to us? I think it's exactly like that. It's a good visual for one of the many ways we can view the Holy Spirit. In Acts 1:8, Jesus says to the disciples, "You will receive power when the Holy Spirit comes on you; and you will be my witnesses…to the ends of the earth." The Holy Spirit, as part of the triune God, sanctifies our lives, transforming us into all we can be in Jesus.

When I think of the first men who were given the Holy Spirit (the disciples), I think specifically of the transformation of Peter. In Acts, we see the boldness of Peter numerous times; "Then Peter stood up with the Eleven [disciples], raised his voice and addressed the crowd" (Acts 2:14), or in verse 40, "With many other words he [Peter] warned them; and he pleaded with them, 'Save yourselves from this corrupt generation.'" In Acts 4:13 it says the people saw "the courage of Peter," and in verse 33, "With great power the apostles continued to testify to the resurrection of the Lord Jesus."

This was the same Peter who had cowered and denied knowing Jesus to a servant girl when she asked if he was Jesus' disciple (John 18:16–17). Peter's courage and boldness came only after Jesus went to heaven and the Holy Spirit entered in. Before his death, Jesus told the disciples, "It is for your good that I am going away. Unless I go away, the Advocate will not come to you; but if I go, I will send him to you" (John 16:7). The *cape* of the Holy Spirit couldn't be put on unless and until Jesus went away.

What about us? How do we put on the cape? We accept Jesus'

death on the cross and his resurrection thereafter. We ask him into our hearts as our own personal Savior, and we repent of our sins. Then, and only then, are we saved "through the washing of rebirth and renewal by the Holy Spirit, whom he poured out on us generously through Jesus Christ our Savior" (Titus 3:5–6). We are born of the Spirit like my so-called wacky relatives revealed to me all those years ago. The Spirit is within us, guiding, giving, and groaning as we "become heirs with hope of eternal life" (Titus 3:7).

Throughout Acts, we see the strength, boldness, and power of the disciples because of the cape of the Holy Spirit, a power which had not been present before the death and resurrection of Jesus. The promised one was not yet within them.

How can we be like the disciples? How can we have strength and boldness and power? After all my words to this point about lures and threats, warnings, and deceptions, I want you to know that without the Holy Spirit's cape of power and protection, strength is impossible to accomplish. We can't do a darn thing on our own. We must be "clothed with garments of salvation and arrayed in a robe of righteousness" (Isaiah 61:10). Romans 8 speaks to our life in the Spirit as it tells us we will have life and peace and power. We should seek, ask, and wait on the Lord. He will not withhold from us what has already been given to us.

## DO YOU WANT THE CAPE?

Do you want the power of the Holy Spirit in your life? Do you want the cape? Does the idea of being like the disciples, having the cape of boldness and courage, frighten you? Don't let it. Let the power of the Spirit change you the way it changed Peter and the disciples and all the saints. The way it changed me. I didn't publish my first book or start speaking until I was sixty years old. I didn't put myself out there with my faith until then. Obviously, I wasn't ready. God was refining and growing my boldness (and my knowledge of the Word) as he continues to do. This isn't an overnight process for most, not that God can't thrust anyone at any time into being a bold witness. Just don't let the idea overwhelm you. We are all growing in courage and righteousness, and God gives us what we need at the time we need it. "For the Spirit God gave us does not make us timid, but gives us power, love and self-discipline" (2 Tim. 1:7).

## HOW TO ASK FOR THE CAPE

How do we ask for the cape? We start with our belief in Jesus. We accept Jesus as our Savior, repent of our sins, and are born of the Holy Spirit. We are sealed with him. Ephesians 1:13–14 (ESV) says, "In him you also, when you heard the word of truth, the gospel of your salvation, and believed in him, were sealed with the promised Holy Spirit, who is the guarantee of our inheritance until we acquire possession of it, to the praise of his glory."

And then we seek the Spirit out in our daily lives through Scripture and prayer. One of the best ways to remind us of the basics of our faith is to pray the way Jesus instructed us to pray:

"Our Father in heaven, hallowed be your name, your kingdom come, your will be done, on earth as it is in heaven. Give us today our daily bread. And forgive us our debts, as we also have forgiven our debtors. And lead us not into temptation but deliver us from the evil one" (Matt. 6:9–13).

The more you know the Word, and walk in its authority, the more you'll find yourself listening, hearing, and responding to the Holy Spirit. You'll know you're wearing the cape. Paul says (Rom. 9:1–2), "I speak the truth in Christ – I am not lying, my conscience confirms it through the Holy Spirit – I have great sorrow and unceasing anguish in my heart."

The Spirit speaks to us. He "teaches and reminds us of everything Jesus has told us" (John 14:26). Anything which does not give testimony to the truth of the Word is not and cannot be from the Spirit. He comes to testify only to truth and that truth is God's Word. 1st John 3:6 (ESV) says, "No one who abides in him keeps on sinning," and (v. 9), "No one born of God makes a practice of sinning. For God's seed abides in him; and he cannot keep on sinning, because he has been born of God." The Spirit grieves and groans when we go our own way. He desires our best.

I don't know all the ways the Spirit speaks to us (nor is he limited in his ways), but for me, he prompts verses to my mind on many occasions. I walk and write every morning and it's the Spirit who brings me thoughts of God and the Word and draws me into certain topics and verses.

The Spirit reminds me of the Word to keep me on the straight and narrow. Philippians 4:8, for instance, has become a powerful anti-sin verse for me. I hear a whisper (to my conscience, like Paul) that asks; Is this lovely? Is it noble? Good? Righteous? Valuable? Praiseworthy? Paul also said you can do anything and everything but not everything is beneficial or useful to grow a life worthy in the Lord. These are among the many verses which have me turning away from sin. The more understanding of the Word you have, the more the "Spirit of truth will guide you into all truth" (John 16:13). I'm convinced there are a myriad of ways he works in my life.

You may see this as a legalistic burden, but it is far from it. It is, for me, like the cookies or cake I'm tempted to eat, yet know I must walk away from if I'm to stay healthy. The Holy Spirit is how I recognize my selfishness, greed, jealousy, aimless wandering, impatience, and all things sinful. If I'm tempted to participate in something that's not my best holy self, the strength of the Spirit and the Word within guides me to steer clear. When I turn away, I don't have the burden of having done something unlovely. I don't have to carry guilt or shame or repent of something I didn't do. I don't always do what's right, but the burden of sin's temptation lessens because the Spirit abides in me, and I'm learning how to listen to him. When I turn from sin, I stay in joy.

## PUTTING ON THE CAPE

How do you put on the cape? If you are a believer, you have been born again of the Spirit. If you are born again of the Spirit, you already have the cape. It's on you already. Ask for the power of the cape. Pray over the power of the Spirit within you. Jesus says, "How much more will your Father in heaven give the Holy Spirit to those who ask him" (Luke 11:13).

It pleases God to be asked. He's not hoarding goodness and wisdom. He offers them freely to those who ask and seek them out. Respond in obedience when you are prompted in all things holy. Don't put off reading the Word. Turn from sin. See Jesus in all things. Jesus made it clear how much we need a helper, comforter, and advocate. We need the Spirit.

The Spirit has put eternity on my heart. The Spirit replaces doubt and fear with wisdom and hope. The Spirit keeps me from getting distracted by worldly ways. I rise early each morning. I read the Word, ponder, pray, write, and walk. This is the work of the Spirit in me because it's not the natural me. The natural me would look nothing like the anointed me. The anointed me abides in Jesus, and walks the walk of intentionality, effort, perseverance, denial, love, and faith, and when I stumble, I get back up again. That's the work of the Spirit. I try to remind myself to give credit where credit is due. "This is how we know that he lives in us: We know it by the Spirit he gave us" (1 John 3:24).

Getting dressed in the cape is a metaphor for how I remember I'm clothed in the presence and power of the Holy Spirit. It's the imagery of putting him on, and the reminder that he abides in me, and as such, I have his power in me.

So, from one wacky sister to another, "Honey, are you born of the Spirit?" Will you put on the cape every day, and with the power of the Word, gain the superpower which has already been entrusted to you? Will you give the Spirit his due and let him help you recognize and defeat the challenges that come your way? Will you get up every morning and dress accordingly, and by doing so, let him change your life for the better?

# CHAPTER 15

Bible verse: *Acts 2:14* – Read.
Write out the first part of the verse in the space below:

_______________________________________________

_______________________________________________

_______________________________________________

_______________________________________________

Peter went from weak to strong in the power of the Holy Spirit, and he went from denying Jesus to addressing crowds of people for the purpose of drawing others to Jesus. But Peter wasn't always Peter.

Peter was an unlikely first disciple of Jesus. He was a fisherman. He was Simon before Jesus changed his name to Peter [the rock]. Simon means one who listens and hears. Simon, the fisherman, gave up everything to follow Jesus, and he did it "at once" (Matt. 4:20). The KJV called it "straightway," meaning immediately and without hesitation.

A flawed fisherman, a nobody, becomes best friends with the promised Messiah. God in flesh. It gives me chills to think on it. I have the hope of Jesus in my life, but not everyone I care about has that hope. Not everyone has gone straightway to the Savior.

An author writes for both himself and his reader. This book is, in large part, about me. It's a reflection of my life, thoughts, and journey with God. And, this book is about you, the reader, and your life in Christ, your journey, and your discipleship. However, I'd like this reflection on the redeeming love of Christ and the power of the Holy Spirit, given to and sealed in a nobody fisherman named Simon (and sealed in you and me), to be about someone else.

I'd like you to think of someone in your life who needs the hope of Jesus. Maybe a son or daughter. A parent. A cousin. A friend. You want them to be found. You want them to have the Holy Spirit, like Peter…and me…and hopefully, you.

That person in your life, who seems so far away from knowing and accepting Jesus and being transformed by the power of the Holy Spirit, is one decision away from being saved. One decision away from straightway. One decision that can change their life forever. It is right that we ask the Holy Spirit to draw them in and change their life. Don't give up. Don't lose hope. Don't think God can't work miracles. By the power of one decision and the power of the Spirit, that person can be saved.

So, think of that person and write out a prayer for them to be saved by Jesus and sealed with the Spirit:

> *Lord, to those of us who are saved and privileged to be called your friend, we are grateful and humbled. We commit this reflection to that one person in our life who needs to recognize you as a friend. We pray for them to answer the call on their heart, so, they too will know the saving grace and love that you freely offer. And they too will run, not walk, into your arms straightway… immediately…at once. Yet your will be done. Amen.*

# 16

## Hope Deferred

*I had no choice but to confront my reality.*

Early in my role of being a mom to four daughters, I found myself drowning in the sorrow of my circumstances. Our two newly adopted toddlers had giardia, a resistant parasite which brought diarrhea almost 24/7 for many weeks. I was changing twenty diapers a day while figuring out how to mother little ones who didn't speak the language or know how to be in a family. Our two oldest daughters were homeschooled which brought its own demands on daily life. Getting out of bed each morning was a struggle. Nothing was turning out the way I thought it would. Hope started to drain out of me. It was the closest I've ever been to a rising depression. At my lowest point, I stood in the shower and had a meltdown. I sobbed and sobbed, letting my sadness wash over me. Minutes into that cryfest, I had what felt like an infusion of the Holy Spirit. I don't know what else to call it. I had an experience that changed my attitude and changed my heart, and I was never the same again.

After that, I started rising each morning with purpose. I was determined to honor God with the blessing of our new family of six. My circumstances hadn't changed, but I developed a kind of hope which I had not experienced before. My hope was deferred. Delayed.

I started to hope more in the end of the story than the difficulties of my present circumstances.

When I considered final challenges to defeat the threats to a strong faith, I was brought back to the book *Good to Great* by Jim Collins, which I read almost twenty years ago. There's a section in the book called "The Stockdale Paradox." This paradox says, "You must maintain unwavering faith that you can and will prevail in the end, regardless of the difficulties, and at the same time have the discipline to confront the most brutal facts of your current reality, whatever they might be."[16]

The paradox refers to Admiral Jim Stockdale, a prisoner-of-war in the Vietnam War. He was terribly tortured and imprisoned for eight long years. The question Jim Collins asked Admiral Stockdale, in interviewing him for his book, was, "How did you deal with your horrible circumstances when you were in the midst of them?" Admiral Stockdale said, "I never lost faith in the end of the story. I never doubted, not only that I would get out, but also that I would prevail in the end and turn the experience into the defining event of my life, which in retrospect, I would not trade."

Admiral Stockdale spoke of the prisoners who didn't make it out. He called them "the optimists." He went on to explain that the optimists were the ones who put deadlines on their expectations of when they were going to be released. Christmas. Easter. Thanksgiving. With each holiday's passing and one more disappointment of not being released, they lost hope. He told Jim, "You must never confuse faith that you will prevail in the end – which you can never afford to lose – with the discipline to confront the most brutal facts of your current reality, whatever they might be." Admiral Stockdale ended by saying, "They died of a broken heart."

*They died of a broken heart.* They didn't confront the most brutal facts of their current reality. For those of us who have gone through (or are going through) something that may or may not have an earthly resolution…like a debilitating illness, the loss of a child, or the

---

[16] Collins, Jim. 2001. Good to Great. Harper Collins. Pages 83-87 (encompasses all quotes)

breakup of a marriage, we need to first "face the brutal facts of our current reality," and then, "have faith that we will prevail in the end." Why? In order to have and keep hope, stay the course, and not wither or die of a broken heart.

## HOPE IS OUR STRONGEST ASSET

Hope is a powerful motivator and an anchor in the Christian faith. If we are to have faith in what is unseen (Heb. 11:1), then we must also have hope in what is unseen. Faith and hope. Are they different? Yes, they are. Faith has to come first. You must believe in something in the present before you hope for it in the future. In the midst of crisis, hardship, or loss, hope becomes the secret to continuing on without faltering. It's worthy for us to consider because hope is easily lost, especially when our hope is placed in earthly deadlines and earthly gains.

One of the clearest verses of hope (for me) is found in Paul's declaration in Philippians 1:21, "For me, to live is Christ, and to die is gain." If we live, we have Christ. If we die, we have Christ. To live and die is the same, yet not. If we die, we gain Christ. If we live, we have Christ *and* we have the hope of Christ. It is faith and hope of something great to come.

Paul also said, "I desire to depart and be with Christ, which is better by far" (Phil. 1:23). *Better by far.* Let's be honest. Hardly any of us would consider it better by far to die. I'm not ready to leave my family. Yet as I get older, I relate to Paul's proclamation. I'm at the tip of understanding how being with Jesus is going to be better than what I have now, as well as knowing I can trust God to provide for my family when I'm gone.

I grow in the hope of things I can't see as the Word's truths grow in me. It's why I've more recently longed for Jesus' return. I have asked God, in the midst of the world's evils, "When is Jesus coming back?" often wondering why it hasn't happened yet. I have prayed for Jesus' return. This can only be the work of the Spirit in me because I can't conjure that kind of longing and hope on my own. It's not natural. What's natural is for me to want to be with Mike, my girls, and my grandchildren, and live forever.

## WHAT IF YOU'VE LOST HOPE?

Hope keeps our spirit alive, and without it, we are crushed. If you've gone through illness, divorce, loss, or trauma, it can feel hopeless. Perhaps you feel crushed in spirit because you're floundering without purpose. Or you feel hopeless, not knowing why you feel hopeless. You don't have to have something bad happen to feel a loss of hope. Loneliness and hopelessness are a pervasive condition of our culture. Its prevalence reportedly grows more each year. Whether a result of a terrible event, or aimless wondering and loneliness, temporal earthly hope will not and cannot sustain you until the end.

John Piper said in one of his videos, "Facts change emotions."[17] What facts? The hope and encouragement of God's Word? The Spirit's uplifting presence? Jesus' redeeming death on the cross and the covenant he has with those who believe? The Bible says from the beginning of time to the end of time, God and his Son are the ultimate hope, and they (and hope) will prevail in the end.

## JESUS IS FAITH AND HOPE NOW

How do we hold onto hope? Admiral Stockdale said it so well, even if he wasn't speaking about godly hope; "You must maintain unwavering faith that you can and will prevail in the end, regardless of the difficulties, AND at the same time have the discipline to confront the most brutal facts of your current reality, whatever they might be."

Let's change one word to make it relevant to our faith:

"You must maintain unwavering faith that *Jesus* can and will prevail in the end, regardless of the difficulties, *and* at the same time have the discipline to confront the most brutal facts of your current reality, whatever they might be."

Doesn't this change everything for those of us who believe in Jesus and his promises?

We still have a responsibility to confront hard circumstances. I

---

[17] https://www.desiringgod.org/messages/greatest-book-greatest-chapter-greatest-joy

stood sobbing in the shower all those years ago, wishing away my problems, until the Spirit showed me that God loved me, my hardships weren't going away, and to stop feeling sorry for myself, *and* do the hard work that needed to be done. I had no choice but to confront my reality. When I did, I was able to face my reality with faith that God knew, and he would make everything right in his time. The hope that God would make everything right is the hope I've clung to for more than twenty years.

We can't wish away our circumstances, take our woes to the bottle, seek comfort in the wrong places, and think our problems are going to take care of themselves. We must cling to the fact that Jesus *can* and *will* prevail in the end. In fact, he's already won and claimed the victory. "But take heart! I have overcome the world" (John 16:33). Jesus *has* overcome the world. It's already been accomplished.

The biggest threat we have to a strong faith is a lack of hope within our circumstances. To be clear, I don't have hope because everything in my life is smooth sailing. I have unresolved issues, the greatest being the estrangement with our adopted daughters (as of this writing). Yet my hope isn't in the resolution of those relationships (even as I want them to be resolved). It's in Jesus, the perfecter of my faith. If I die tomorrow without a resolution, I'll be content to leave the outcome in Jesus' hands. I don't have to see or know exactly how he will "work it all out for good." I don't have to see each grandchild come to know the Lord. God loves them more than I do, and I trust he will seek a relationship with each of them. My hope is in Jesus, not in the success of whatever outcomes I want.

## FREED FROM THE THORN

Besides Jesus, Paul is a great example of maintaining faith no matter what and still acknowledging the difficulty.

Paul had a thorn…something painful (unnamed).

He prayed (the Bible says *begged*) three times for it to be removed.

God answered by *not* removing it.

Paul continued on in his ministry despite the thorn.

He lived with the pain of the thorn.

He discredited the thorn by never mentioning it again.

His love for Jesus grew.

His ministry to others was powerful.

He spread the Gospel exponentially.

Paul tells us clearly why he continued in his faith and ministry so valiantly; "I consider that our present sufferings are not worth comparing with the glory that will be revealed in us" (Rom. 8:18). He goes on to say we will be "liberated from decay and brought into freedom and glory with God" (Rom. 8:21, paraphrased). Guess what? Paul is liberated from his thorn. He no longer has to suffer with it. Isn't that amazing?

Can we be like Paul? Can we maintain unwavering hope in Jesus, live with our thorns without wallowing, and carry on with a life devoted to loving Jesus and making disciples? Can we dare see Jesus as more valuable than what life throws at us?

## PURPOSE IN THE PAIN

To move on, we follow Paul's example. We pray for God to remove the pain, but we don't put our hope in the pain being removed, which means we accept the answer if it is no. We thank God for the pain (because he must have a purpose in it). We minimize the importance of the pain as we place God over and above it. We use the pain to serve and minister to others, although it's not a badge to be flaunted. It's not for our boasting. Jesus is our source of strength and the only one in whom we boast. Finally, we see that our pain is temporal, not eternal, which is why we can withstand it. We will one day be liberated from it.

Specifically, how do we do this? Anchor yourself in the Word. Pray continually. Seek a strong faith-filled community. Trust in the Spirit's guidance. There's nothing that will bring you and your spirit down quicker than surrounding yourself with hopelessness. That includes the people around you, what you watch, read, and put into your mind. Your mind is pliable. It has the propensity to shift downward if you are not careful.

There are many books of the Bible that speak to hope in Jesus. Romans and Hebrews are among my favorites. Hebrews 6:18–19 says, "It is impossible for God to lie…we are to take hold of the hope set before us and be greatly encouraged. We have this hope as an anchor for our soul, firm and secure. It enters the inner sanctuary behind the curtain, where our forerunner, Jesus, has entered on our behalf." Hope for the believer is about the what, not necessarily the when or the how or even the why. Hope in what? Hope in Jesus. God's Word is filled with the right kind of hope which leads to the right kind of strength in God.

This kind of resolve and strength and hope is for those who believe in Jesus. Those who don't know Jesus Christ as their Savior hope only in those things which will make them happy. People manage their lives in order to manage their happiness. Charles Spurgeon, in one of my favorite-ever sermons states, "Happiness is a thing that depends upon how things happen. It is too often hap-ness, and nothing more. It is too much a hap-hazard thing. But faith rests in Christ whatever hap may happen; and so it is happy in the happening of sorrow and grief, because it relies wholly upon God."[18]

Our life in Christ is for holiness to prevail. Hope in a person. Hope in an eternal outcome, no matter the cost, no matter the time it takes. Hope in being united with our Savior when it's all said and done. Hope in joy's final destiny. Sometimes I fear the pain of things to come, and yet I still hope. I still have joy. I try not to get ahead of myself.

The best feedback I received at one of my retreat talks was when a woman told me, "I love how much you've been through, yet you still praise God." I want to live up to this statement. I want to still praise God no matter what. The ultimate hope I have is hope in the ending, an ending I can't see but has been promised to me. It's the kind of faith I pray for despite what's happening around me.

"Though the fig tree does not bud and there are no grapes on the vines, though the olive crop fails, and the fields produce no food, though there are no sheep in the pen and no cattle in the stalls, yet I

---

[18] https://www.spurgeon.org/resource-library/sermons/little-faith-and-great-faith

will rejoice in the LORD, I will be joyful in God my Savior. The sovereign LORD is my strength" (Habakkuk 3:17–19).

I will rejoice in the Lord. I will be joyful in God my Savior. I will. Because Jesus has already prevailed.

# CHAPTER 16

Bible verse: *1 John 5:13* – Read.
Write the verse in the space below:

_______________________________________________

_______________________________________________

_______________________________________________

_______________________________________________

Hope deferred is not hope lost. Deferred, by definition, means delayed for or until a stated time. Later on. Not now. We are a culture trained to think in the here and now which makes waiting difficult for us. We wait for very little, and that's not changing anytime soon in a culture gaining more and more expediency and immediacy each and every day.

We are tasked to live in the here and now as Jesus tells us, "Not to worry about tomorrow" (Matt. 6:34, emphasis added), yet we are also tasked with putting on an eternal lens for our hope of forever. That's hope (in earthly outcomes and resolutions) deferred, and the kind of hope we need to develop. We must commit to the idea that we have something more than this life to look forward to.

What kinds of things do we worry about? Why do we worry so much?

Explain why the concept of eternal hope is difficult to absorb into our practical lives?

Read and ponder Romans 6:1–14.

Did you notice these phrases?

"We too may live a new life."

"United with him [Jesus] in a death like his."

"United with Jesus in a resurrection like his."

"Our old self crucified."

"Our body ruled by sin is done away with."

"No longer slaves to sin."

"Set free."

"We will also live with him [Jesus]."

"Alive to God in Christ Jesus."

"From death to life."

"Under grace."

Is Romans 6 talking about now, tomorrow, or eternity? YES. As believers, we are alive and united in Christ, our old selves crucified and not ruled by sin. We are set free. We have come from death to life. Now and forever.

Romans 6:22–23 – "But now that you have been set free from sin and have become slaves of God, the result is eternal life. For the wages of sin is death, but the gift of God is eternal life in Christ Jesus our Lord."

The result is eternal life when you accept Jesus into your heart and are sealed with the Holy Spirit. What we think of as deferred hope becomes today's hope and it starts to change how you see the world and your circumstances…from here to eternity.

> *Lord, you've given us so much to think about in the area of hope. We are living in a world where hope seems lost. People are lonely and depressed and overcome by their feelings and their circumstances. For those who know you, our hope is deferred to being with you in eternity, but also to being with you right now. All praise for this amazing truth. Yet your will be done. Amen.*

# 17

# A Worthy Promotion

*Sometimes I miss the point.*
*I think with my head and not with my heart.*

There's something a counselor said many years ago that sticks in my thoughts as I write this last chapter. She commented on my stoicism and my lack of sentimentality. She said I could be more "warm and fuzzy" towards my youngest daughter. I had practiced endurance, calmness, and dispassion for so many years in an effort to protect myself when crisis came, I didn't know how to be anything else. I didn't know how to be *emotional*. Even writing the word makes me cringe a bit. If my younger daughters went into an aggressive or screaming tirade, I kicked into a kind of deadpan stoic resolve, belying the fear and anxiety I felt underneath that resolve. I couldn't lose control. I was the mother after all. What was I supposed to do? Cry? Scream? Hit? Throw? Go crazy? Break down? I didn't have it in me.

When it came to raising children with RAD (Reactive Attachment Disorder) and ODD (Oppositional Defiant Disorder), I survived by planning and strategizing. I perfected tough-mindedness. I rose with intention. I had a daily plan, even when it came to my emotions. I couldn't let the issues of the day throw me off my game or be my demise. I had to stay the course.

My entire life's training has been about discipline and endurance. My early training in sports and music prepared me for the long hard road of dealing with attachment trauma. I was made to be their mom. I knew how to deal with hard things and survive. I did not wilt. I did not go catatonic. I stayed the course, determined to rise above my circumstances. Strategy and tough-mindedness helped get me through.

Strategy and tough-mindedness are why I've remained healthy since my wellness conversion seven years ago. I drew the boundaries, and although those boundaries get tweaked with new insights about nutrition (nor am I perfect), I stay the course. Someone recently told me she never knew anyone who aged backwards like I have. Our over-processed, over-indulgent world is not an easy place to stay healthy yet resolve and patience have helped me remain so.

Strategy can be a good thing, but we can't let strategy be front and center in our faith. Faith is not a strategy. Jesus is not a plan. He is a person seeking our hearts and our feelings in all the depths he created them to be. So, it is with this lead-in that I write this chapter, because sometimes I miss the point. I think with my head and not with my heart.

## FAITH IS ABOUT THE HEART

The Bible talks about the heart significantly more than it talks about our minds. It's our heart God is after, a heart which seeks Jesus and trusts in his promises. Faith, the Bible says, is only faith because of things unseen. Faith is a feeling as it is a choice. Psalm 40:8 (NLT), "I take joy in doing your will, my God, for your instructions are written on my heart." Joshua 24:23 tell us to "yield our hearts to God."

I've had to work at the feeling side of me. I've had to work at being more vulnerable, more emotive, and less like a Pharisee – one who loves and studies the Word but doesn't love to the full that God intends. "Warm and fuzzy" doesn't always come naturally to me, yet I'm learning to dive deeper into my feelings because I believe it's the desire of God for me to have an invested, yielded, feeling heart towards him and others. What about you? What is the state of your heart?

## WWDD

Remember the 1990's when the WWJD trend was widespread? It was a re-ignited saying from a book written in 1896 by Charles M. Sheldon, *In His Steps: What Would Jesus Do*. I suspect it started rightly, but I always thought the focus tended more towards our behaviors of attributes like kindness, giving, and love than on the person of Jesus. Also, at times, it felt somewhat counterproductive as I knew I couldn't attain Jesus-likeness. I'm not negating the trend. Anything that puts focus and awareness on Jesus is ok with me.

I find it more relevant in my life to ask WWDD. What would David do? David, was after all, the one called a "man after God's own heart." Why is David the one after God's own heart? David didn't always have stellar behavior and in fact, did some awful, sinful things. Yet despite that, God still singles him out as having his heart. What does that mean? Does it mean David had a lifelong pursuit chasing the heart [feelings] of God, or does it mean God felt a deep connection with David? What does it mean and how can we be a people after God's own heart?

David was different from his people, the Israelites. Both the Israelites and David had troubles and they both sinned, but Israel was always being forced *by* God into a relationship *with* God. David, on the other hand, was always seeking an intimate relationship with God. Israel consistently turned away from God and David consistently turned towards God. There's a distinct difference. They both sinned, but their sin led them in opposite directions. Their hearts were different. David loved God from the depths of his heart. Israel loved Israel.

While Jesus is our example of a perfect life and perfect love, David is our example of an imperfect life *and* deep love and longing for God. The Psalms are a study in David's feelings. He wrote things like:

"I thirst for you, my whole being longs for you."
"Because your love is better than life."
"I will sacrifice with shouts of joy."

"I cling to you."

"I am deeply sorry for what I have done."

"I love you Lord, my strength."

David felt deep emotions. He loved. He desired. He longed. He mourned. David wrote in all his feelings. It's easy to forget he was a powerful warrior king when you read his beautiful poetry of love, devotion, and longing.

David "danced before the LORD," and not only did he dance, but he danced "with all his might," and he did it "wearing nothing but a loincloth" (2 Sam. 6:14, emphasis added). Frankly, I'm embarrassed by David's practically naked dancing. I can't imagine dancing with all my might before God, clothed or not.

## A REFLECTION OF GOD

David is a whole-hearted feeler and I struggle to relate. I'm too sensible. I don't think I have it in me. I'm more a Martha than a Mary. I serve more than I sit. I study and write more than I pray. I talk more than I listen. I like to have a task and get it done. Yet I want to be more like David. I want to love with his kind of abandonment. I want to be able to sit with the Lord and be still. I want to cling to God with all that I am.

What about you? Have you considered whether you are a lover or a doer? A Martha or a Mary? A woman after God's own heart like David? Can you dance or sing or praise God with all your might? Or worse yet, simply sit and be still before the Lord? Try that one on for size.

It isn't just David's feelings we see in the Psalms. In Psalm 40:11 (KJV), David calls God's mercies tender, as he says, "LORD, don't hold your tender mercies back from me." David could have just said, don't hold your mercies from me, but he called them tender. We are reminded over and over again of God's feeling nature towards us.

David was a man after God's own heart, not just because of his faith and loyalty to God, but because his heart was filled with the capacity for deep emotion. There was no stoicism, no neutrality, and no protective shell over his heart. No one could accuse David of not being "warm and fuzzy." Because of the depths of his feelings, we see both the character of David and the character of God reflected *in* David. It's a beautiful witness of who we are meant to become in our walk with God.

## A LOVING MINISTRY

What about Jesus' three-year boots on the ground ministry? We clearly see the love Jesus had for others, especially in the way he allowed himself to be consistently interrupted by the needs of those around him. Jesus didn't just pass by those in need. He saw people for who they were, and when he did, he stopped, loved, and ministered to them. He demonstrated his care and love in surprising and unique ways to each person. What we know of Jesus and his care of others is what we read in the Bible, but John tells us, "Jesus did many other things as well. If every one of them were written down, I suppose that even the whole world would not have room for the books that would be written" (John 21:25).

Jesus is "the same yesterday, today, and tomorrow" (Hebrews 13:8). He is our Savior, Mediator, Advocate, and Master Shepherd. He died for our sins, not because of a strategy, but because of love. The kind of love that feels, suffers, cries, is vulnerable, and gives up his life for another. It's mind-boggling to consider.

## THE HEART DECLARES THE FATHER

Jesus said in John 14:21, "Whoever has my commands and keeps them is the one who loves me. The one who loves me will be loved by my Father, and I too will love them and show myself to them." Notice what it doesn't say. It doesn't say, "Whoever keeps my commands will go to heaven." It says that by our actions we show our love, and it is followed by whoever loves me will also be loved.

What comes first? Do we keep the commands, or do we love God? The point is they go hand-in-hand. They aren't meant to be independent of one another because if we don't love the Lord, we won't do what is right by him, nor will we have the sustenance to know and abide in the truths in God's Word. Love is the sustenance. It is the means by which we carry forward.

God's instructions are "written on the heart." What good does it do if our hearts aren't invested in God's instructions? What good does it do if our behaviors are perfect, yet we have no love? It does no good. 1 Corinthians 13:1 says, "If I speak in the tongues of men or of angels, but do not have love, I am only a resounding gong or a clanging cymbal. If I have the gift of prophecy and can fathom all mysteries and all knowledge, and if I have a faith that can move mountains, but do not have love, I am nothing. If I give all I possess to the poor and give over my body to hardship that I may boast, but do not have love, I gain nothing."

What good would it do if I write a dozen books, speak, and serve but am not filled with love for Jesus, and love and longing for others to be saved and sanctified? Fill in your own blank: What good would it do if ____________________________, but do not have love?

So, which is it? Do we give our feelings a worthy demotion, or a worthy promotion? Do we subjugate them rightly or do we seek the depths of them? It's less about demotion or promotion, and more about developing a heart for Jesus. That's what David did. He practiced a heart of integrity and love. "God chose David his servant and took him from the sheep pens; from tending the sheep he brought him to be the shepherd of his people Jacob, of Israel his inheritance. And David shepherded them with integrity of heart; with skillful hands he led them" (Psalm 78:70–71).

What does "integrity of heart" mean? It means his heart was right before God. We should be like David. Practice shepherding with integrity of heart. Dance with abandon before the Lord. Long for the lover of our soul. Praise and bless our Father in good times and bad. Learn to be still with him. Learn to love and feel the way he has created us to love and feel, reflecting his character when we do so.

I want to be a strong woman of God and the Word, but more than that, I want to love my Savior well. I want to walk with him and talk with him and know I'm loved by him. I want his voice to be like no other voice within me. That's my prayer for all of us.

## "In the Garden"[19]

*He speaks and the sound of His voice*
*Is so sweet the birds hush their singing;*
*And the melody that He gave to me*
*Within my heart is ringing.*
*And he walks with me,*
*And he talks with me,*
*And he tells me I am his own,*
*And the joy we share as we tarry there,*
*None other has ever known.*
*None other has ever known.*

---

[19] C. Austin Miles, author/composer

# CHAPTER 17

# Study and Reflection

Bible verse: *1 Corinthians 13:13* – Read.
Write out in the space below:

_______________________________________

_______________________________________

_______________________________________

_______________________________________

I don't want any of us to miss the point. I don't want to get through this book or any book and miss the love. We can so easily get caught up in the *doing*. Our faith and discipleship aren't in the doing. They're in the loving. Love God. Love others. If we do nothing else, this is who we are to be and what we are to *do*.

Paul, the writer of the letters to the people of Corinth makes sure we don't miss the point, and 1st Corinthians 13 is the best "love" chapter for this. There's a reason this verse is used in marriage ceremonies. I urge you to read chapter 13. It says if we don't have love, we have nothing.

Paul wrote all of his letters to followers of Jesus, and each letter differed based on the dynamics of the group. Paul's "love letter" to the people of Corinth was written because they needed to be reminded, just like we need to be reminded.

Paul was not always a lover. In fact, Paul was a hater before his conversion to Christianity. Read Acts 7:57-8:3 where we are introduced to Paul (first known as Saul). He approved killing. He destroyed the church. He "dragged off" Christian men and women and put them in prison. In Acts 9:1, it says, "Saul was still breathing out murderous threats against the Lord's disciples." Saul was a hater through and through.

Yet here he is, talking about love. It was only by an act of God that Paul was converted, saved, and became a lover with a desire for all to know and love Jesus. That is a true conversion of the heart. God chose Paul. Jesus saved him. The Holy Spirit convicted him. He went from hater to lover.

What about you? Would you call yourself a lover and if so, what does that look like?

My word of the year has been "deference." Look up and define the word deference:

Did you find words like submission, respect, kindness, yielded, consideration, patience, and regard for others? In thinking about this idea of deference, it occurred to me how little of it we see. Deference to others in a store. Deference to your spouse or a friend. Deference to someone at work. Deference to neighborhood children. Deference to waiting.

I think love looks like willing and joyful deference. Putting others first shows a heart of kindness and love. It shows a willingness to put yourself lower than others and be happy in the lowering. Deference means giving up expectations of a me-first life.

The conversion of our lives to Jesus is not a functional conversion based on tasks and activities. It's a conversion of spirit and heart and I don't want us to miss this. It's a willing deference of the heart to love and lift others up above ourselves. In the end, love's all we got!

> *Lord, we commit this chapter and this verse to you. Thank you for the conversion of one of our greatest witnesses and lovers, Paul. He shows us what it is like to have gone from hate to love. He is our example of loving others and having a willing heart to bring others to know Jesus. Give us the same willingness to defer our lives to others in the name of Jesus Christ, our Lord and Savior. Yet your will be done. Amen.*

# EPILOGUE

## The Frailty of a Foreigner

*They all stared at me. I wanted to crawl under the table.*

I was at a party recently, when the conversation around the table turned to discussing the Koran and world religion. My interest was piqued as I listened to everyone's views. One woman said, "If people would just follow the golden rule, we wouldn't have any problems in this world." The group agreed, and the consensus around the table was that religion is a "very bad made-up thing."

In that moment, I was not compelled to speak up, but God forced my hand. The host turned towards me and said, "Sheri, don't you write about these kinds of things?" I was instantly caught off-guard as she exposed me for the foreigner I was, putting me on display for all to behold. I diverted my eyes down, long enough to take a breath and grasp at a response.

"Yes, I do write about things like this," I reluctantly breached my silence, "In the Bible [there, I said it], there *is* a kind of golden rule and it's called dying to yourself."

"What?" the first woman said, a little too dismissive for my comfort.

"It's called dying to yourself," I repeated, more forthright, "Dying to your own wants, needs, and desires so you can attend to another's needs and desires the way Jesus did, because so often serving others means denying yourself."

They all stared at me. I wanted to crawl under the table. "That sounds rather harsh, don't you think?" the woman scoffed. With all eyes turned back on her, a new subject, golf, was quickly introduced and my metaphorical dying was thankfully over.

I knew in that moment I had played it safe. I didn't give away too much. I said only enough to reveal my faith, but not so much as to expose the truth I carry inside me. "Jesus is the way and the truth and the life. No one comes to the Father except through him" (John 14:6 – paraphrased). This truth, however, is not the claim I made that day. I said just enough to keep things nice and tidy. I commented on the golden rule. I didn't give Jesus away like I could have.

How often do I feel tongue-tied like Moses, want to flee like Jonah, or worse yet, deny like a young Peter? I look nothing like the strong John the Baptist or the forthright Paul. I am passionate about Jesus, and yet, I wither under pressure. I'm fragile. I recognize this in me, and I dislike my weakness. Oh, how the devil revels in my weakness. I chide myself for my inadequacies, pray for grace, and ask the Spirit for the ability to do better next time. Next time. I'm sure there will be a next time. There always is. A next time to be unashamed of the Gospel. 2nd Timothy 1:7-8 tells us, "For the Spirit God gave us does not make us timid, but gives us power, love, and self-discipline. So do not be ashamed of the testimony about our Lord."

I know, however, even before my weakness is revealed in me, I'm forgiven and embraced by my Savior. I want to be courageous, but even when I'm not, I'm no less loved.

*"Oh, that I had the courage of Great-heart, that I could wield his sword and be as valiant as he! But, alas, I stumble at every straw, and a shadow makes me afraid. Listen, Little faith. Great-heart is God's child, and you are God's child too; and Great-heart is not one whit more God's child than you are. Peter and Paul, the highly favored apostles, were of the family of the*

*Most High; and so are you also; the weak Christian is
as much a child of God as the strong one."*[20]

The weak Christian is as much a child of God as the strong one.
Thank God for the grace of Jesus. Thank God I'm still a child of God
in and through my times of weakness.

My five-year old granddaughter recently said to me, "Grammy,
I like being at your house because you treat me like a princess." I
laughed and beamed. That child doesn't always act golden, nor do
the others, but as a grandparent, it's easy to treat them all as princes
and princesses. I love them from a place I didn't even know existed
within me. That's how Jesus loves me. Like no other. I'm a princess
in training; a royal heir to the kingdom (Luke 12:32, Rom. 8:17),
despite my inadequacies and disobedience, my fragile faith, and faltering courage.

The frailty of me is also the strength of me. Had I not answered
in a manner I considered weak, I wouldn't have thought about it for
most of the hour drive home. I wouldn't have called Mike and talked
it out with him. I wouldn't have prayed over it, nor practiced a better
answer for another time of being called to the witness stand. My moment of weakness was used to strengthen me.

"No man can have too low an opinion of his own power; because
he has no power whatever. The Lord Jesus Christ said, 'Without me
ye can do nothing,' and his witness is true. If we have strong faith we
shall glory in our powerlessness, because the power of Christ doth
rest upon us. The weakest faith is real faith."[21]

The comfort in my soul is that God didn't need me to save anyone
at that party. He's perfectly capable of saving those he chooses to save.
God is solely in charge of reaching the lost, thank goodness. I can also
trust that my words, even in their weakest state, can, and will make
an impact on others.

We don't need to beat ourselves up over our inadequacies. We
don't need to condemn ourselves for being fragile, weak, incompe-

---

[20] Morning and Evening. Charles H. Spurgeon. 1995. Hendrickson Publishers, Inc.
p. 156.
[21] https://www.spurgeon.org/resource-library/sermons/little-faith-and-great-faith

tent, awkward, and *seemingly* ineffectual. And it's up to us to remember that *the weak Christian is as much a child of God as the strong one.* I am confident in my position as a saved daughter of the King.

"The God of all grace, who called you to his eternal glory in Christ…will himself restore you and make you strong, firm, and steadfast. To him be the power for ever and ever. Amen" (1 Peter 5:10-11).

What about you? Are you fragile? Do you read a book about lures and threats and feel it all a burden? Are you overwhelmed with everything you can't do, rather than focusing on what you can do? Are you like a young Paul who was frustrated by the things he could and should be doing in the name of Jesus?

It's really ok. "Whoever believes in him is not condemned…" (John 3:18). If God is not looking to condemn you, you shouldn't either. God seeks to mold, refine, and grow your faith and he'll use any means necessary, even your own frailty at a dinner table of lovely, albeit lost souls, who think that following the golden rule is the way to save the world.

"For you were once darkness, but now you are light in the Lord. Live as children of light" (Eph. 5:8).

No weakness or faltering can hide the light of Jesus and the Spirit in you. Live your light, and when you do, don't be ashamed. Move quickly past your frailties. Don't dwell in them. Dwell, instead, in the loving arms of the Father who has brought you thus far and will continue to do so until you are united with Jesus. By your weakness, his strength will be revealed and made perfect. Go live your weakness foreigner.

# ACKNOWLEDGEMENTS

To Mike, whose love and constancy grounds me. Thank you for continuing to support my ministry of writing and speaking and for being invaluable for final line editing. I couldn't do this without you.

To Susan Spivey, thank you for continuing to work through my chapters with me. I learn something new every time we're together. I'm blessed by you.

To Janyre Tromp, thank you for making my 2nd developmental edit as educational and seamless as the first one was. I'm so grateful you're on my team.

To Roseanna White, thank you for the beautiful cover design, and helping me format and publish the book. You are as rock solid professional as they come.

To Cyndi Alioth and Kathy Sassaman, thank you for believing in me to teach my first ever written Bible study at West Shore Free using content from both *Challenged* and *Strong*. Looking forward to increasing and strengthening the sheep in our fold.

To West Shore Free Church, I'm grateful for a church filled with Bible-believing, truth-telling, nurturing, shepherding, and loving people, and being my home base for more than twenty-five years.

To God, "who arms me with strength and keeps my ways secure… who makes your saving help my shield…who provides a broad path for my feet so I will not slip" (2 Sam. 22:33, 36, and 37).

# ABOUT SHERI WALKER

SHERI WALKER, and her husband Mike, live in South Central Pennsylvania, where they've been for more than thirty-five years. They have four daughters and six grandchildren. At sixty-one years old, Sheri's experienced quite a bit of "life." She's been a choir and worship pianist and singer, home stager, homeschool mom, realtor, sales trainer, Bible study leader, writer, and speaker. Although it feels like she's still figuring it all out, her sixties have been the best, most fulfilling years ever, and in many ways, she's just getting started.

Sheri has experienced deep heartbreak and loss. She lost her mother in 2001 to breast cancer. She and Mike experienced the loss of four babies through miscarriage, and together, they've journeyed more than 20 years with the aftereffects of orphanage neglect and trauma of their two adopted daughters. In 2016 and 2017, Sheri suffered a brain tumor which left her paralyzed on her left side before the tumor's successful removal six months after discovery.

At 61, Sheri is physically healthier and stronger than she's been in years, but more importantly, she's been transformed by the Holy Spirit to know and love Jesus more deeply and bring others to know him more deeply. She has a heart for believers to develop strong biblical stewardship, know what godly purpose and calling looks like, and stay focused on generational mission and eternal hope.

Over the years, Sheri and Mike have mentored parents of behavioral-challenged kids and been involved with a non-profit organization to combat trafficking all over the world. Sheri is also the author of *Strong, From Here to Eternity*, and her next book, *Called, From Here to Eternity* will be out spring 2025. She is available to speak at churches, conferences, retreats, and small groups.

You can find more information on her books and speaking at
www.sheriwalker.com.

# ABOUT FROM HERE TO ETERNITY SERIES

Why *From Here to Eternity* as a series? The Bible says much about heaven and eternity, and it's valuable to filter our lives accordingly. All the topics I explore within a strong faith walk have been filtered through eternal hope.

Paul said (to Timothy) in 2 Timothy 1:5, "I am reminded of your sincere faith, which first lived in your grandmother Lois and in your mother Eunice and, I am persuaded, now lives in you also."

I love this verse. It's simple but powerful, and it makes me think of my grandparents who were my first faith models. I want to be like them, and like Lois, as I look to hand faith down to my family and others, even the ones who will never know my name. Let this encourage all of us to know that our faith is our greatest and only legacy that matters.

What about your legacy? Are you seeing it through an eternal lens? Will you be like Lois and pass on a strong faith to others? I'm hopeful this series will help you do just that.

Thank you for your interest in this series. I look forward to hearing your stories of strength and how the Spirit is moving in your life and the lives of those around you…from here to eternity.

Your friend in Christ, Sheri